To my mother Thérèse, my beautiful children Sylvie, Chantelle, Marc, Luc and my dedicated husband Gerry — thank you for all your support.

Thank you especially to Gerry for making my dreams come true as usual, and for all the practice sessions to make this book the very best that it could be.

*MC Thauvette*

# HONEYMOON
# PLAYBOOK
### Your guide to "scoring" the best romantic honeymoon ever!

# Acknowledgments

Thank goodness for daughters and their great supportive friends!

I am grateful to my daughter Sylvie Paquette-Lussier and her friend Selena Lake for coming up with this book's highly creative name when I was stumped. Sylvie's introduction to innovative and stylish book designer Nathalie Cloutier was another saving grace. The stunning photos are thanks to photographer Robin Andrew and photo models Jennifer Janes and Kevin Bird, Brittany Clark and Gabriel Tesfaye and Dina-Désirée Papiccio and Dominic Papiccio. Many thanks to portrait photographer Roger Sands. This book wouldn't look half as gorgeous without my book design dream team!

I have my other daughter Chantelle Thauvette and her best friend Alia Martin to thank for deep dives into key themes during discussions in the hot tub, cocktails in hand. Cheers, ladies!

It truly takes a village to write a book: thank you to Taylor Holmes for her suggestions, support, and attention to detail as the general editor of this book; To my copyeditor Erin, thank you for your final touches. To my assistant and great friend Cathy for her encouragement. To Elena, Angie, Amy Kimmick, Laurel Johnson, Sophie Tsourus: thank you for your creativity, patience and support. I am also forever appreciative of my friend and creative sister, Dee. Thanks to my art teacher Jenny, I finally know how to draw a fairly decent penis and vulva.

I am deeply grateful to an inspiring group of women in my MULTIgenerational Mastermind Sexual research team: Angela Koskie, Emily Walsh, and Sophie Tsourus. I promise with the success of this book our next meeting will be at Le Nordik Spa!

Thank you to Roz Dishiavio, my AASECT supervisor and ISEE teacher for giving me my favorite learning experience of all time as a sexual education student. Thanks to all my ISEE classmates.

For welcome distractions and inspiration, I am thankful for my sons Luc and Marc, granddaughters Gabrielle and Nicole, and newest grandson, Théo. Big thank you to my number one cheerleader and positive mom that made me promise she would get the first copy of *Honeymoon Playbook*.

Thank you to my students and clients, whom I continue to learn from.

The communication and sexual activities in this book have all been kitchen and bedroom tested with my husband of twenty years, Gerry. Thanks for appreciating and enjoying all those sexual experiments. Now we will get to kick it up a notch for the second book! Maybe next time our research can take place on a remote Caribbean island.

The *Honeymoon Playbook* is a thoroughly delightful book. MC Thauvette really knows how to make having fun on a honeymoon easy, with ready-made "his" and "her" activities both in bed and out. The author is a gifted certified sex educator who has been running workshops and seminars for male-female couples for years. She brings her in-depth knowledge of communication and sexuality to bear, pairing it with creative ideas that are destined to bring a sense of play and discovery to the early-marriage experience. Easy to read, fun to use, this book is a fabulous gift idea for showers or weddings, too.

– **Dr. Rosalyn Dischiavo**, author of *The Deep Yes, the Lost Art of True Receiving*

# REVIEWS
## FOR THE HONEYMOON PLAYBOOK

This is exactly the kind of practical, playful, down-to-earth approach that modern sex education needs! Marie-Claire captures the importance of a holistic approach to relationships, where communication is just as important to your sex life as the saucy tips and tricks. I absolutely loved reading and exploring the variety of exercises and games. There is something for everyone here, and I've never been more excited to do my "homework"!

– **Emily Walsh**

The *Honeymoon Playbook* is full of brilliant tips, tricks, games and exercises that bring couples together, both emotionally and physically. As a couple's counselor and sex therapist, I believe working through this book can help couples avoid many relationship pitfalls that bring them to therapy later in their relationship. Learn more about yourself and your partner using questions you never thought to ask!

– **Anne Mauro**, MA

This is a "one-of-a-kind" book! Once I started reading, I could not put it down as I discovered page after page of wonderful and very exciting ideas, tips, and suggestions. This is a book I will reference for years to come.

– **Dr. Krista Richard**

# A LETTER FROM THE AUTHOR

While writing the first draft of this book, I got extremely motivated by visualising thousands of couples on their honeymoons engaging in exciting conversations and activities to improve their relationships romantically and intimately. It brings me great joy to think that this book will make a difference to newly married couples (and even not so new) and help them build a deeper connection with each other.

Planning a wedding is often stressful and time consuming. From choosing flowers, being subtly exclusive with the guest list, making amicable seating plans, picking the cake topper, and saying yes to the dress or suit, there is hardly any time or energy left to plan a memorable honeymoon! Your honeymoon is one of the most important trips of your life, and you deserve to have the best possible experience.

That's where the *Honeymoon Playbook* comes in! The activities in this Playbook will light a romantic fire in you and your spouse that will last longer than any vacation tan. For the best possible effect, read this book before your honeymoon as well as during. Anything you don't do on your honeymoon can be saved for another trip or tried at home.

This *Honeymoon Playbook* includes games, techniques, activities, suggestions, and checklists. All of the ideas in this book can be modified to suit your relationship (and your honeymoon)—it's all about you, after all. I strongly encourage you to mark this book up. Fill in the blanks, and make notes in the margins. After your honeymoon, you can and should use this as a reference to look back on. If one of you is shy or skeptical, have the other one act as the leader for some of the sections. You don't have to do things in order. Look through the Playbook, and decide where it feels most playful to start. Getting started is the key!

Get out of your comfort zone and really connect with your spouse on an intimate level. Keeping a sense of humor will soothe any anxieties you may have, and keep you laughing and connected until you are in your retirement. That is the goal of this book: to make your first trip as a married couple a powerfully enjoyable experience that you will remember forever. The focus is less about sexual intercourse and more about playing together. The Romance and Foreplay sections are just as important as the Sex section!

Do not hesitate to reach out to me personally if you need any support. My goal as your couples coach is to help deepen your romantic connection and provide you with ideas for a lasting and loving marriage. As an AASECT Board Certified Sexual Educator and relationship coach, I am here to help you on your honeymoon journey and beyond. You can contact me through my website (relationshipbliss.ca).

Now let the honeymoon planning and fun begin!

With love,

MC Thauvette

# A Win-Win Game: How to Use This Playbook

## Before You Leave

- Skim through the entire book before your honeymoon to see which activities and games appeal to you the most. Try some if you are adventurous!

- Decide how you want to use this book, e.g. read together or separately, mark sections, etc.

- Consult the packing list on pages 174-176 and tips for adventure travel on pages 168-173.

  **Note:** Although this book is divided into Romance, Foreplay, and Sex sections, the intent is to focus less on the actual act of intercourse and more on having fun together and building a deep and long-lasting connection.

## While You're Away

- Dig into whatever tickles your fancy at that moment. Don't feel you have to go through this book in any order.

  ° Feel like talking? Check out pages 10 to 50 in the Romance section.

  ° Feel like being teased and touched? Try the sensual massage activities in the Foreplay section on page 94.

  ° Want to explore? Give the sexual blueprint activities a go in the Foreplay section on page 99.

  ° Want to try something new or adventurous? Play one of the sexy games in the Sex section on page 130.

- Don't be afraid to mark this book up! Write notes on the lines provided, and if you need more room, fill in the margins too! Write down your thoughts, memories, and notes.

  - It is meant to be used as a reference guide long after your honeymoon, so the more you write, the more you'll get out of this book.

- This Playbook is your Playbook; customize it to your relationship and experiences. You don't have to follow the games and activities exactly if they don't appeal to you. Missing something for one of the games? Improvise and be creative!

- If you or your partner is experiencing any sexual issues, check out pages 164-165 for possible solutions or see a sex therapist.

## When You Return Home

- Review all your notes and try some of your favorite activities again.

- Meet regularly afterward (e.g. monthly) to review your notes and keep your honeymoon spark alive!

- Check my website or Facebook page for more exciting sexual bliss and play ideas. (relationshipbliss.ca)

## The Right Equipment:
## What You Need to Get Started

Although there is a complete trip checklist in Appendix B, there are a few key things you will need to complete the activities in this book that you may not have thought of packing.

### Lubrication

Many of the activities and games in this playbook suggest using lube or oil for safety and comfort.

- **Lube:** an all-natural, water-based lubricant is recommended. It is much less sticky than silicone-based lubricants and is safe to use with all sex toys. Silicone-based lubricants can damage silicone sex toys and make them unsafe to use.

- **Oil:** virgin coconut oil is the safest (and sexiest!) oil option. It is usually solid at room temperature, but can easily be melted by scooping some out and rubbing it quickly between your hands.

**CAUTION: DO NOT use coconut oil (or any oil) with latex condoms:** It will degrade the latex and can cause the condom to break. If you are using condoms, use an all-natural, water-based lubricant.

### Sex Toys

You may be limited by luggage space, so the following smaller-sized sex toys may be preferred.

- **A small bullet vibrator:** A bullet vibrator is no larger than your finger but can be very powerful.

- **A sleeve or stroker toy:** A toy for him in the Pleasure Anatomy Plays on page 111. The stroker or sleeve fits around the shaft of the penis.

### Specific Items You'll Need for the Activities

Your Sexual Blueprint (page 94)

- Two large poster rolls or pieces of newspaper end roll long enough to trace each other's body for a fun little romp. Use thin newsprint style paper so it can easily roll or fold into your suitcase. (Can't fit this? There is a mini outline in Appendix C you can use.)

- Colorful markers. (You can do this activity without markers, but markers are so much more fun!)

Sensual Massage for Newlyweds (page 99)
- A feather or a ticklish item like a soft brush

Sexy Games (page 130)

- **Kissing Cards:** deck of cards and one spoon.

- **The Newlywed Game with a Twist:** paper, pen, soft neckties, two hats or creative containers.

- **Slippery Wrestling:** a plastic sheet (shower curtain works), nontoxic and nonstaining foam or paint, underwear you are not attached to.

- **Indoor or Outdoor Water Fight:** two water guns, two white T-shirts.

- **Hide and Ice:** two blindfolds, lingerie for her, and sexy underwear for him.

- **Nerf® or Sock War:** one Nerf® gun and ammo or five socks rolled up into balls.

# ROMANCE

Your guide to "scoring" the best romantic honeymoon ever!

# ROMANCE

Many people associate romance with grand gestures such as expensive dinners by candlelight, bathtubs filled with rose petals, or extravagant public displays of passion—thanks Hollywood! Although these expressions of love can be fun and exciting, they are not always practical or easy to plan and deliver. Day-to-day romance is the key to a deep and lasting connection. It is all about knowing your partner and truly making an effort to understand and appreciate the way they need to be loved.

But isn't your honeymoon automatically romantic? Not necessarily! Both of you need to make an effort to make it memorable; true romance doesn't happen on its own. How can you put day-to-day romance into practice on your honeymoon? It can be via activities, events, or gestures that are meant to acknowledge your partner's desires, enhance their joy, and bring a sense of connection. Romance requires releasing your own ego to connect with your partner. Rather than a one-size-fits-all approach, think of romance as unique to your relationship and your spouse's needs.

For example, sunglasses are not inherently romantic, but if your spouse forgets, loses, or breaks them, then buying them a new pair and presenting them along with a handwritten note becomes an act of romance—simple as that. Or perhaps, if your partner is an adrenaline junkie and you prefer quieter activities, agreeing to try that helicopter tour would be an act of romance.

You likely already realize that romance is one of the crucial components of all successful marital relationships. It takes effort and observation to ensure it stays strong. After getting married, you may find that how you romance your spouse and how you feel about being romanced changes. You've just made a huge commitment to each other, after all! A commitment like marriage can lend your relationship more stability and trust. You may feel more comfortable branching out and trying new things together or making longer-term plans. There is no better time to start exploring those new feelings than on your honeymoon, or anytime you need an extra spark in your relationship.

How can this Playbook help? The games and activities in this section are designed to encourage romantic behaviors in both you and your spouse with the goal of bringing you closer. What you learn through these activities will help create a more intense connection and afterwards you will have wonderful honeymoon memories. You will also develop romantic habits that will continue to benefit you both.

This section includes:

- Daily Sweet Surprises

- Making Future Plans Together

- The Appreciation Game

# Pre-game Warmup: Daily Sweet Surprises

Your honeymoon shouldn't be like any other trip. An easy way to make it extra special is to surprise your spouse (yes, spouse, you're married now!) every single day of your honeymoon. The surprise doesn't have to be an elaborate gift, but it should be special to them.

## What to Get?

You don't have to spend a lot of money; thoughtful gifts from the heart are often the most meaningful. Remember to pack light and keep the gifts small, particularly if you are travelling by plane.

## Is Your Spouse an Early Bird or a Night Owl?

If they are a morning person, surprise them with a gift at breakfast or put it on top of a freshly made bed before they come out of the bathroom.

If they are a night owl, offer their gift at supper or put it on their pillow before bedtime, so you are their last memory before they close their eyes.

For an extra dose of fun near the end of your honeymoon, hide the gift. Get your partner to look around while you direct them with instructions like "you're getting hotter" or "oops, getting cold" until they are on top of you. Perhaps the gift is hidden in your pocket, or maybe you are the gift!

**BRIDES:**

Skip to page 18! NO PEEKING!

**GROOMS:**

Keep reading. This section is full of ideas on daily sweet surprises to give to your wife.

# Gifts for Her (Brides: DO NOT READ!)

**Buy her jewellery:** Check out the jewellery your wife already owns to get a sense of what style of earrings, necklaces, or bracelets she prefers. When in doubt, try to match the piece to her favorite dress or top. Tip: Hide the jewellery in a pair of your socks so she doesn't accidentally find it.

**Pick her flowers:** Pick a bouquet of local wildflowers. Every time she sees the beautiful blooms in the room, she'll be reminded of your sweet gesture. If you do not have access to wildflowers, an exotic bouquet will leave a lasting memory. (If your wife loves fruit or chocolate, arrange for a platter of these instead! Remember to take lots of photos to preserve these memories.)

**Find her a quirky keepsake:** Purchase a small memento, or better yet, find one on a beach or a nature walk during your trip for her to bring back home.

*"I found these beautiful, large, unusual, and HEAVY rocks on one of our trips, and without me knowing, my husband went back and picked them up for me, and get this, he carried them for almost two kilometres! They are now in our pond at home, and every time I look at them, I remember that special, romantic gift."*

**Surprise her with a thoughtful present:** Planning an excursion, but she forgot to pack something? Buy it for her as a gift to use during the day's excursions, and attach a note explaining how excited you are to spend the day with her.

**Make her queen for a day:** Tell her that she gets to stay in bed and have fun all day! There is just one rule: she is only allowed to get up to eat, drink, bathe, dance, take bathroom breaks, and spend time with you. Be at her beck and call, and really make her feel important. This is also a great opportunity to practice some activities from this book. Ask her questions about herself, and get to know your new wife on a deeper level. Tip: get room service or delivery so you never have to leave the room!

**Prepare her a Honeymoon Goodie Bag:** Include all her favorite things like her most loved chocolates, crossword puzzles, gum, card games, nail polish, jewellery, and hair accessories in a beautiful bag. You can ask one of her bridesmaids or friends with amazing creative taste to help you with this project. You could also include fun props or toys that will inspire some creativity in the bedroom!

**Woo her with poetry:** Write her a spontaneous poem on hotel letterhead and leave it on her pillow. If you'd rather not pen the poem yourself, buy a poetry book, or look online, and transcribe one of your favorites (always giving credit to the true poet!). To up your game, read poems to her aloud that remind you of her. If poetry seems like a daunting task for you, write a sentence or two about why you love her, and leave it for her in a private place.

**Surprise her with an activity:** Try something new together that you know she will enjoy, such as a fun excursion or lesson. Here are some ideas:

- Horseback riding

- Ethnic cooking class

- Dance lesson

- Scuba diving or snorkelling

- Paddling (canoe, kayak)

- Orienteering

- Hiking

- Wine tasting

- Bartending

- Stand up paddleboarding

Many all-inclusive resorts offer interesting workshops that really are dynamic and worthwhile. Find out what is available and surprise her.

Bring a secret sex toy on your honeymoon. As you climb into bed (or in the morning before your day begins), tell her that the theme is pleasure! Snag a toy in advance at your favorite adult toy store, wrap it, and present it to her as a gift at that special moment. Have her coach you on how to use it on her. Ask her to give you one-word directions such as slower, faster, up, down, softer, harder, etc. If she is the silent type, ask her to moan loudly when you have hit the best spots!

*"Be sure to make a healthy toy choice: buy a phthalate-free toy. **Big, important tip:** Be sure the toy is fully charged before the trip, or bring batteries!"*

**Book a couple's massage:** Remember this is her gift, so be sure to get her the massage therapist with the touch that is right for her. Ask if she prefers a light, medium, or deep massage, a male or female therapist, and if she would prefer seeing you massaged by a man or a woman.

**BRIDES:**

Keep reading. This section is full of ideas on daily sweet surprises to give your husband.

**GROOMS:**

Skip to page 22! NO PEEKING!

## Gifts for Him (Grooms: DO NOT READ!)

**Appreciation journal:** Pick up a blank journal or one that includes a calendar with space for writing, and write a dedication to your husband, explaining that you vow to find something that you appreciate about him every day for thirty days. Then, do exactly that! Write a short note describing one small thing you appreciate about him in the journal every day and leave it for him to read daily.

**Sexy underwear:** Buy some sexy—not lingerie—underwear for HIM! Let him know how sexy he is in them, and exactly what you plan on doing to him after you strip them off.

**Burlesque surprise:** Bust a move burlesque style! Set up some sexy music in your room and get dancing. Men are visual creatures, so be confident in yourself.

**Boudoir photo book:** Get some professional photos taken in your sexiest outfits, and have the best ones made into a discreet photo book to present to him on your honeymoon. This will require planning before your honeymoon. Not only will this create endorphin inspired confidence in you, but it will also create a solid visualgasm for your husband.

**Wash him:** Tell him that he is a very dirty boy, then suds him up in his favorite scent (nothing too girly!). Get creative—try to wash him using different parts of your body before using your hands to give him a teasing wet massage.

**Favourite food or drink:** His favourite nosh or libation may not be available where you are going, so bring it with you! Put his favourite beer on ice, or bring a shot glass to toast with a nip of whiskey or other liquor.

**Four-hand massage:** This is something he will never forget! Find a massage therapist that won't mind you joining in on the massage. How it works is the massage therapist is on one side, and you are on the other. You are their mirror as you follow their lead. Be sure to notice his pain and pleasure spots (but not those special ones... yet!), and the pressure and speed used. You will become an expert masseuse in no time!

*"This will be an unforgettable experience: My husband and I did this when we first met, and it was love at first four-hand! This was a bonding experience for us, and after twenty years, we continue to take, and mutually enjoy classes."*

**Surprise him with an activity:** Try something new together that you know he would enjoy; schedule a fun excursion or lesson during your honeymoon. Here are some ideas:

- Zip lining

- Parasailing

- Wakeboarding

- Fishing

- Paddling (canoe, kayak, or Stand up paddleboarding)

- Hiking or cycling

- Wine or spirits tasting

- Lingerie shopping

- Spa treatment

- Wake boarding

- Cooking class

- Cigar lounge

- Professionnal race venue (eg. car or horse)

## Surprises Gifts: Checking In

Answer the following questions by filling in the blanks below.
Be specific! For example: "I loved the burlesque surprise!
Her confidence was so sexy."

What was your favourite "sweet surprise" from your honeymoon
and why?

Mrs.:

_____

_____

_____

_____

Mr.:

_____

_____

_____

_____

*"Check in with your spouse to see what future
activities or gifts they might enjoy for your second
honeymoon."*

Now, go back over the sections together. Were there any surprises from your spouse's section that you especially liked? What appealed to you about them?

Mr.:

_____
_____
_____
_____

Mrs.:

_____
_____
_____
_____

*"I recommend that you keep the adventure and fun flowing your whole married life. Meeting once a month to make adventure plans will help you to feel alive as a couple."*

## Team Huddle: Making Future Plans Together

Newlyweds, even if you were together for a long time before you tied the knot, will still benefit romantically and sexually from wedding excitement. You should bask in that excitement—you're husband and wife now! However, without new experiences together most couples become too accustomed to each other and can easily fall into a humdrum routine. Psychologists at *The American Psychology Association* say that couples who incorporate novelty, variety, and surprise into their lives can rekindle the passionate feelings they experienced when they first began their relationship.

Couples who have conversations about their hopes, dreams, and fears—not just daily household matters—experience higher relationship satisfaction. Talking about the water bill is hardly the basis of romantic daydreams, after all. Dr. Terri Orbuch of the University of Michigan theorizes that couples who converse about personal values and dreams create shared meaning and purpose in their relationships. Having conversations about future plans, fears, needs, values, and desires on your honeymoon will help keep those meaningful dialogues going and give you a road map for keeping the excitement alive in your marriage.

The following questions are divided into sections based on traditional marriage vows. You can tackle the questions at once, or do one question from each section at different times. How you go through the exercise is entirely up to you. It is very important to ask these questions when you are both in a calm and happy state of mind with no time constraints. It might be good to do these in the morning before you start your day or at night before bed depending on your schedules. If you are stuck on a question that gives you difficulty, move past it to the next question, and come back to the first question later.

Try taking turns reading the questions and writing down your partner's answers. Do one question and then switch! For example, if "Mr." reads the question, he writes his wife's answers on the "Mrs." line. Read the answers back to each other to ensure you have understood and documented them correctly. Taking notes may seem like a lot of trouble, but you need to capture key thoughts for future reference.

## To Have and to Hold

How many cuddle times would be ideal for you?

Mrs.: _____/week

Mr.: _____/week

How long would you like to cuddle each time?

Mrs.: _____/minutes

Mr.: _____/minutes

How much foreplay time would you enjoy?

Mr.: _____minute(s) hours: _____

Mrs.: _____minute(s) hours: _____

How many times per week would you enjoy being sexual with each other in some way?

Mrs.: _____/week

Mr.: _____/week

## For Better or for Worse

If we had a special cocktail party to share our honeymoon photos and experiences with our closest friends and family, how do you think we could make it special? (For example: what kind of food, drink, and music could we prepare to make the theme unique to our honeymoon?)

Mr.:

_____
_____
_____
_____

Mrs.:

_____
_____
_____
_____

What would you like to do to celebrate our anniversaries in the future?

Mrs.:

_____
_____
_____
_____

Mr.:

_____
_____
_____
_____

How would you like to celebrate our BIG anniversaries?

**Ten Years**

Mrs.:

_____
_____
_____
_____

Mr.:

_____
_____
_____
_____

**Twenty-Five Years**

Mr.:

_____
_____
_____
_____

Mrs.:

_____
_____
_____
_____

## Fifty Years

Mrs.:

_____

_____

_____

_____

Mr.:

_____

_____

_____

_____

As a married couple, would you like us to host theme night dinners or parties? (e.g. an 80s night?)

Mrs.:        Yes ◯        No ◯            Mr.:        Yes ◯        No ◯

If yes, what would be your favorite themes to try?

Mr.:
1. _____
2. _____
3. _____

Mrs.:
1. _____
2. _____
3. _____

What are three adventurous things you would like to do together?

Mrs.:

1. _____
2. _____
3. _____

Mr.:

1. _____
2. _____
3. _____

What sports, activities, or hobbies would you like to do together?

Mr.:

1. _____
2. _____
3. _____

Mrs.:

1. _____
2. _____
3. _____

What can we do in our area that would be really fun?

Mrs.:
1. _____
2. _____
3. _____

Mr.:
1. _____
2. _____
3. _____

Who would you prefer us to see if we encounter problems in our marriage that we can't solve ourselves? (e.g. therapist, relationship or sex coach, clergy, trusted family friend?)

Mr.:

_____
_____
_____
_____

Mrs.:

_____
_____
_____
_____

# For Richer or for Poorer

What are three small preferred physical presents you would like to receive? (e.g. flowers, tools, pens, paper, books.)

Mrs.:

1. _____
2. _____
3. _____

Mr.:

1. _____
2. _____
3. _____

What gift of time would you like to receive? (play games, board games, baths or showers together, dance, cuddle, make love, etc.)

Mr.:

1. _____
2. _____
3. _____

Mrs.:

1. _____
2. _____
3. _____

What are the top three things you would like to save money towards (e.g. trip to the Caribbean, Porsche, house.)

Mrs.:

1. _____
2. _____
3. _____

Mr.:

1. _____
2. _____
3. _____

If money were no object, what activities together would you prefer? For example, eating out with friends, a romantic dinner out, entertaining friends at home, or a romantic dinner at home. Give your preference in percentages by coloring in the provided circle.

For example, your pie chart may look like this!

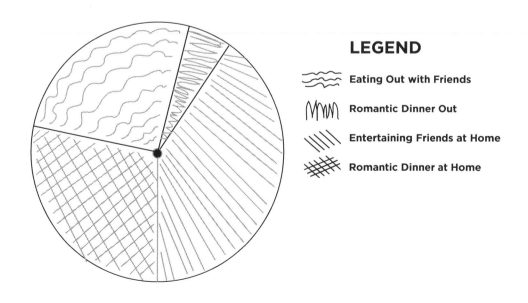

**LEGEND**

〜〜〜 **Eating Out with Friends**

ᴍᴍᴍ **Romantic Dinner Out**

\\\\\\ **Entertaining Friends at Home**

▨▨▨ **Romantic Dinner at Home**

Mrs.:

Mr.:

## LEGEND

 Eating Out with Friends

 Romantic Dinner Out

 Entertaining Friends at Home

 Romantic Dinner at Home

## In Sickness and in Health

What situations at work (if applicable) stress you and drain your energy?

Mrs.:
1. _____
2. _____
3. _____

Mr.:
1. _____
2. _____
3. _____

Name three things you would like your spouse to do to help you de-stress from a hectic day:

Mr.:
1. _____
2. _____
3. _____

Mrs.:
1. _____
2. _____
3. _____

What situations at home stress you and drain your energy?

Mrs.:

1. _____
2. _____
3. _____

Mr.:

1. _____
2. _____
3. _____

Name three things you would like your spouse to do to help you de-stress at home:

Mr.:

1. _____
2. _____
3. _____

Mrs.:

1. _____
2. _____
3. _____

What else is stressful to you and drains your energy?

Mrs.:
1. _____
2. _____
3. _____

Mr.:
1. _____
2. _____
3. _____

Name three things you would like your spouse to do to help you de-stress from the above.

Mr.:
1. _____
2. _____
3. _____

Mrs.:
1. _____
2. _____
3. _____

What would you like your spouse to do when you are sick to make you feel better?

Mrs.:

1. _____

2. _____

3. _____


Mr.:

1. _____

2. _____

3. _____


## To Love and Cherish

If you want to improve your faith or spiritual life, what actions would you like to take, and what can your spouse do to support you?

Mr.:

_____

_____

_____

_____


Mrs.:

_____

_____

_____

_____

Would you be willing to schedule a weekly date night together?

Mrs.: Yes ◯ No ◯  Mr.: Yes ◯ No ◯

If no, why not?

Mrs.:

_____
_____
_____
_____

Mr.:

_____
_____
_____
_____

If yes, what do you think those dates would look like?

Mr.:

_____
_____
_____
_____

Mrs.:

_____
_____
_____
_____

What makes you happy and makes you laugh?

Mr.
Happy:

_____
_____
_____

Mr.
Laugh:

_____
_____
_____

Mrs.
Happy:

_____
_____
_____

Mrs.
Laugh:

_____
_____
_____

## From This Day Forward

How many children do you want?

Mrs.: _____          Mr.: _____

What are your three favorite names?

Mrs.:
1. _____
2. _____
3. _____

Mr.:
1. _____
2. _____
3. _____

What sports, hobbies, or activities would you like our kids to try?

Mr.:

_____
_____
_____
_____

Mrs.:

_____
_____
_____
_____

Do you envision our kids attending private or public school and why?

Mr.:　　　　private school ◯　　　public school ◯

Why:

_____

_____

_____

Mrs.:　　　　private school ◯　　　public school ◯

Why:

_____

_____

_____

If and when we have children, what are some specific things we could do to make time for each other? (e.g. plan regular date nights, quality weekly time together.)

Mrs.:

_____

_____

_____

_____

Mr.:

_____

_____

_____

_____

What family routines did your parents establish in your household? What would you do the same and what would you do differently? Explain.

Mr.:

_____
_____
_____
_____

Mrs.:

_____
_____
_____
_____

Who would you turn to in your life to support you emotionally, other than me, if you needed it?

Mrs.:

_____
_____
_____
_____

Mr.:

_____
_____
_____
_____

What goals or objectives do you want to accomplish as a couple in the next five years?

Mr.:

1. _____
2. _____
3. _____
4. _____
5. _____

Mrs.:

1. _____
2. _____
3. _____
4. _____
5. _____

## Team Cheer: The Appreciation Game

You love your spouse, or you wouldn't have married them! But, in stressful and busy times, it can be easy to forget all the little things that made you fall in love with them in the first place. Your honeymoon is the perfect time to appreciate and highlight all those things. This short activity is meant to remind you of some of those unique things. Document the warm feelings these questions stir up now, so you can enjoy them after your honeymoon is over.

Take turns asking the questions below and writing down each other's answers.

When we first met, what were your first impressions of me?

Mrs.:

_____
_____
_____
_____

Mr.:

_____
_____
_____
_____

When did you decide I was the one you wanted to marry?

Mr.:

_____
_____
_____
_____

Mrs.:

_____
_____
_____
_____

What habit or personal quality do I have that you love the most?

Mrs.:

_____
_____
_____
_____

Mr.:

_____
_____
_____
_____

What is your favorite outfit of mine?

Mr.:

_____
_____
_____
_____

Mrs.:

_____
_____
_____
_____

What is your favorite thing that we do together?

Mrs.:

_____
_____
_____
_____

Mr.:

_____
_____
_____
_____

What is your favorite thing that I say to you?

Mr.:

_____
_____
_____
_____

Mrs.:

_____
_____
_____
_____

What is your favorite memory with me?

Mrs.:

_____
_____
_____
_____

Mr.:

_____
_____
_____
_____

Describe where and when we had our first kiss.

Mr.:

_____
_____
_____
_____

Mrs.:

_____
_____
_____
_____

What has been your favorite event or vacation we've taken and why?

Mrs.:

_____
_____
_____
_____

Mr.:

_____
_____
_____
_____

What is your favorite cute or endearing quality of mine?

Mr.:

_____
_____
_____
_____

Mrs.:

_____
_____
_____
_____

## Romance Recap

Romance takes effort, but it's worth it! Romantic activities will help you to create and sustain a more intense and longer lasting connection. In this section, you learned that:

- Small, thoughtful gifts or gestures can go a long way toward building a strong relationship.

- Talking about your future together aligns your expectations.

- Rereading this section later in your lives will remind you of why you originally loved each other.

- Appreciating and cherishing what you love about your spouse is a cornerstone of romance.

# FOREPLAY

Your guide to "scoring" the best romantic honeymoon ever!

# FOREPLAY

Most women need a lot of foreplay to really enjoy sex, and men can heighten their sexual experience (and maybe go crazy) with more anticipation! Foreplay can start long before you get to the bedroom: leave a teasing note on the bathroom mirror, gently touch your bottom lip while keeping eye contact with your spouse, brush their thigh under the dinner table, or whisper in their ear as you dance sensually. The pace should be like a Sunday drive, not the Indy 500.

If you feel out of touch (pun intended!) and unsure where to start, try the activities in this section. Building anticipation gets the creative and romantic juices going.

## Manage Your Expectations

Many men believe that oral pleasure is foreplay, but for many women, it is the main act and their favorite way to reach orgasm. In a recent report by Dr. Laurie Mintz, she shared a study she conducted at the University of Florida where 95% of women reported that clitoral stimulation is the most reliable way for them to achieve orgasm.

Asking for what you desire during foreplay will not only enhance your experience, it will also make you feel genuinely connected.

## Show Each Other

If you have discovered the touch you prefer through masturbation, don't be shy about sharing that valuable information with your spouse. Getting to know your partner's preferences, and practicing it on them is part of the fun! Experienced couples continually learn about each other's tastes and preferences by trying new things, and what better way to learn than by watching and practicing.

Use sex toys like a vibrator to heighten each other's senses, or heighten them manually. The important part is to show your spouse exactly how you like to be touched. Think of it as a sexy show and tell!

## Lube, Lube, and More Lube

Stress, anxiety, medication, and alcohol can interfere with a woman's natural lubrication production and sexual enjoyment. Foreplay can make a huge difference in offsetting that potential problem. Keeping things nice and wet will make everything much more enjoyable for both of you, so don't skimp on lube if natural lubrication isn't enough. Use an all-natural, water-based lube—nothing with scents or sweeteners—to avoid a potentially itchy or painful reaction.

## Safe Word

Safe words aren't just for the kinky crowd. A safe word is a way for a couple to build trust. You can both feel secure knowing your partner will tell you immediately if something is painful or uncomfortable. Many couples choose to use the stoplight system:

**Green:** Everything is great! Keep going.

**Yellow:** I'm reaching my limit; you should slow down or be careful.

**Red:** STOP EVERYTHING IMMEDIATELY. I am in pain or distressed in some way.

Other couples select a single word that is entirely unrelated to sex (such as a fruit or cooking tool). Yelling "pineapple" in the middle of sex will definitely stop things in their tracks, and could turn a possible awkward moment into a fun one!

Using a safe word doesn't necessarily have to kill the mood. If both of you are up for it, continue your play with the same or another fun activity.

## More Than Touch

Foreplay is considered anything that turns you on. So, how can this Playbook help? The games and activities in this section are designed to get your "turned on" juices going!

This section includes:

- Hot Conversation Starters

- How to Be a Pro Kisser

- Your Sexual Blueprint

- Sensual Massage for Newlyweds

## Game Plans: Hot Conversation Starters

According to research, most romantic partners have difficulty telling each other what pleases and displeases them sexually—even if they have been married for decades. But when couples do talk about sex, they typically report higher sexual and overall relationship satisfaction. Talking about sex doesn't have to be stressful.

Use these hot conversation starters to help get your communicative juices flowing. Your honeymoon is the perfect time to talk about sex; there are no distractions from the outside world, no pressure or scheduling constraints, and plenty of time to act on what you learn.

Asking each other these questions, and writing down the answers will not only help you to know each other on a deeper sexual level, but it will also be a form of foreplay for your honeymoon antics.

Ask each other the following questions, and write down your spouse's answers so you can refer to them later. Like other exercises in this book, it works best when you do them together and take turns. Remember that talking about sex can be foreplay in itself!

Describe three things that make up the perfect kiss.

Mrs.:

1. _____
2. _____
3. _____

Mr.:

1. _____
2. _____
3. _____

What could I do to you sexually on this trip that would make your heart flutter?

Mr.:

1. _____
2. _____
3. _____

Mrs.:

1. _____
2. _____
3. _____

What would be the most enjoyable thing I could do to you during foreplay?

Mrs.:

1. _____
2. _____
3. _____

Mr.:
1. _____
2. _____
3. _____

How would you like me to undress you? For example, slowly, sensually, eyes closed?

Mr.:

_____
_____
_____
_____

Mrs.:

_____
_____
_____
_____

What is your favorite part of my body, and what would you like to do to it if I gave you carte blanche?

Mr.:

_____
_____
_____
_____

Mrs.:

_____
_____
_____
_____

What is the sexiest thing I have ever said to you, or what are the sexiest clothes I have worn?

Mrs.:

_____
_____
_____
_____

Mr.:

_____
_____
_____
_____

What would you say our top three sexual memories are? Get specific: time, place, activity, or sex act.

Mr.:
1. _____
2. _____
3. _____

Mrs.:
1. _____
2. _____
3. _____

Do you prefer the lights on or off while we make love, and why?

Mrs.:

_____
_____
_____
_____

Mr.:

_____
_____
_____
_____


Name three sexual activities you would like to try (or try again!).

Mr.:
1. _____
2. _____
3. _____

Mrs.:
1. _____
2. _____
3. _____

Do you like dirty talk, and if so, what do you like to hear?
(Give some examples!)

Mrs.:

_____
_____
_____
_____

Mr.:

_____
_____
_____
_____

What are your top three favorite sexual positions, and why?

Mr.:
1. _____
2. _____
3. _____

Mrs.:
1. _____
2. _____
3. _____

Name three erotic things you would love me to do to you with my tongue.

Mrs.:
1. _____
2. _____
3. _____

Mr.:
1. _____
2. _____
3. _____

Do you like oral sex, and if so, do you prefer to give or receive it, both, or both at the same time?

Mr.:

_____
_____
_____
_____

Mrs.:

_____
_____
_____
_____

Imagine that tonight you are the boss of me! What are the three things you would have me do to you?

Mr.:
1. _____
2. _____
3. _____

Mrs.:
1. _____
2. _____
3. _____

When you masturbate, what do you do that gives you the most intense orgasm?

Mrs.:

_____
_____
_____
_____

Mr.:

_____
_____
_____
_____

How would you feel about doing a sexy photo shoot to help us remember our honeymoon? If so, what could we do to make it fun?

Mr.:

_____
_____
_____
_____

Mrs.:

_____
_____
_____
_____

How would you feel about "waking up the neighbors" when we make love?

Mrs.:

_____
_____
_____
_____

Mr.:

_____
_____
_____
_____

What kind of dessert would you like to eat off of me, and how would you do it?

Mr.:

_____
_____
_____
_____

Mrs.:

_____
_____
_____
_____

Would you enjoy skinny dipping (swimming naked)? If so, when and where could we do it?

Mrs.:

_____
_____
_____
_____

Mr.:

_____
_____
_____
_____

How would you feel about masturbating alongside me? Would you let me watch you masturbate?

Mr.:

_____
_____
_____
_____

Mrs.:

_____
_____
_____
_____

Would watching me masturbate turn you on?

Mrs.:

_____
_____
_____
_____

Mr.:

_____
_____
_____
_____

What are three foreplay moves you would like to receive?

Mr.:

1. _____
2. _____
3. _____

Mrs.:

1. _____
2. _____
3. _____

What are the three favorite foreplay moves you would like to give?

Mrs.:

1. _____
2. _____
3. _____

Mr.:

1. _____
2. _____
3. _____

Would you prefer to watch porn with me or listen to me read you a dirty story? Give details about the type of porn or story you would most enjoy.

Mr.:

_____

_____

_____

_____

Mrs.:

_____

_____

_____

_____

## Practice Makes Perfect: How to be a Pro Kisser

Kissing is a barometer of your lovemaking skill and style. It's one of the most important components of a long and healthy romantic relationship. A kiss can kick up the heat, communicate love, or simply bring you closer for a brief moment. I recommend including it in all your foreplay activities.

*"Gerry had been filming my kissing workshop, and the whole time I did not think he was listening to the pro-kissing tips. He was! Later on that night in the hot tub, he teasingly came over to my side of the tub, and gave the exact kisses I described to students early on that day. My knees melted. I needed to get to our room fast. I made him promise to never lose his magical touch, and he hasn't."*

Think of kissing as an intense and intimate form of communication that doesn't necessarily have to lead to sex. A deep kiss given with soft lips and loving eyes before asking a partner how their day went, or after a stressful day of travel delays and hotel changes on your honeymoon, is a powerful way to start a loving conversation. A kiss is almost like a conversation without words, and communication is the backbone of a strong and lasting marriage!

This section is all about experimenting and exploring. Get back to the basics, slow things down, and savor each kiss. What does your spouse enjoy, and why? Be sure to spare no detail when you share what you like with your partner; kissing builds excitement for further foreplay, so your spouse needs to know how to give you the kind of love and attention you want.

# His Honeymoon Kisses

**By: Gerry and MC Thauvette**
Gerry and I wrote this poem together.
Try writing your own and cherish it as a keepsake from your honeymoon.

*He looks into her eyes*
*He pauses and smiles*
*He guides his lips to hers*
*He offers his loving touch and kisses her softly*
*He releases his love to her soul*
*She is enthralled*

*He runs his hands through her hair*
*He breathes in her essence*
*He gently guides her head back*
*He kisses her neck passionately*
*He slips his tongue between her willing lips*

*He kisses her until she is lost in his love*
*She is consumed*

*He realizes what he holds*
*He pulls away carefully*
*He cups her cheeks and looks into her eyes*
*He searches for her acknowledgement*
*He sees and feels her desire*
*He kisses her with body and soul*
*She is overcome*

*She releases herself to him*
*He releases himself to her*

## Pregame Rituals: Setting the Mood

- Put on slow, sexy music—the kind that you would both like to slow dance to.

- Dim the lights, or throw a warm-colored (nonflammable) scarf over a lamp.

- Light a few candles for extra romance.

- Brush your teeth, use mouthwash, or chew a stick of gum for a minute or two.

- Slick on a small amount of nonsticky lip balm. Regular unscented Chapstick will do the trick.

- Take the following kissing quiz!

# Tryouts: The Kissing Quiz

This quiz is meant to help you determine what types of kisses you might like to receive. Read the questions under each heading, mark the "yes" circle if you agree with the statement, "no" if you don't agree with the statement, and "maybe" if you aren't sure if you agree or disagree but would like to find out! Once you've finished marking your answers, find where either you or your spouse have circled "yes" or "maybe" and flip to the corresponding kissing section—those are the kisses you should try!

**I like my lips being touched before being kissed.**

Mr.:    Yes  ◯          Mrs.:    Yes  ◯
         No  ◯                    No  ◯
      Maybe  ◯                 Maybe  ◯

Go to **Almost there** page 78

**I enjoy maintaining eye contact while kissing.**

Mr.:    Yes  ◯          Mrs.:    Yes  ◯
         No  ◯                    No  ◯
      Maybe  ◯                 Maybe  ◯

Go to **Tantric Kissing** page 80

**I like to stop mid-kiss to build anticipation.**

Mr.:    Yes ◯          Mrs.:    Yes ◯
        No ◯                    No ◯
        Maybe ◯                 Maybe ◯

Go to **Red Light, Green Light** page 82

**I enjoy adding playfulness and humor to intimate interactions.**

Mr.:    Yes ◯          Mrs.:    Yes ◯
        No ◯                    No ◯
        Maybe ◯                 Maybe ◯

Go to **Playful Lips** page 84

**I like including food into kissing, such as sharing fruit.**

Mr.:    Yes ◯          Mrs.:    Yes ◯
        No ◯                    No ◯
        Maybe ◯                 Maybe ◯

Go to **Playful Lips** page 84

**I like feeling my partner's hands on my body while we kiss.**

Mr.: Yes ◯
No ◯
Maybe ◯

Mrs.: Yes ◯
No ◯
Maybe ◯

Go to **Wandering Hands** page 87

**I like being kissed all over my body between lip kisses.**

Mr.: Yes ◯
No ◯
Maybe ◯

Mrs.: Yes ◯
No ◯
Maybe ◯

Go to **Wandering Hands** page 87

**I enjoy having my fingers sucked and nibbled.**

Mr.: Yes ◯
No ◯
Maybe ◯

Mrs.: Yes ◯
No ◯
Maybe ◯

Go to **Tongue Games** page 89

**I enjoy being pinned against a wall or the bed while my partner kisses me.**

Mr.:  Yes  ◯      Mrs.:  Yes  ◯

No  ◯      No  ◯

Maybe  ◯      Maybe  ◯

Go to **Take me Now** page 91

**I like my hair being tugged during a kiss.**

Mr.:  Yes  ◯      Mrs.:  Yes  ◯

No  ◯      No  ◯

Maybe  ◯      Maybe  ◯

Go to **Take me Now** page 91

## Almost There

Teasing your partner with kisses is a surefire way to increase anticipation. Your partner may think you are going in for a kiss, but—surprise—you do something different! Try these techniques:

- Look at their bottom lip while you lick your own bottom lip. Look up at their eyes briefly while you smile mischievously.

- Dip your head toward them, as if you are going in for a kiss, then do one of the following:
    - Kiss their cheek
    - Kiss their ear
    - Kiss their neck
    - Brush only their bottom lip with yours
    - Place your thumb on their bottom lip

Rate these kisses:     Mr.: _____/10     Mrs.: _____ /10

How did you feel about this kiss? Do you like being teased and if so what did you like best?

Mr.:

_____
_____
_____
_____

Mrs.:

_____
_____
_____
_____

What variations would you like to try?

Mrs.:

_____
_____
_____
_____

Mr.:

_____
_____
_____
_____

## Tantric Kissing

Tantric-style kissing is meant to increase the sexual energy between two people. The most important part of this type of kissing is to maintain eye contact. Try this play series, and switch positions afterwards to let your spouse lead.

**Play 1.** Gaze into your spouse's eyes. Hold their gaze as you move toward their lips with yours. Get close but don't touch them!

**Play 2.** Synchronize your breath with theirs by placing your hand on your spouse's lower belly and feeling them inhale and exhale.

**Play 3.** Bring your hand up to your spouse's chest, and place it flat against their sternum while maintaining eye contact and synchronizing your breathing.

**Play 4**. Lean closer to your spouse's face, and gently lick their top lip.

**Play 5.** Kiss your spouse's cheeks, then forehead, and finally kiss their eyes until they close.

**Play 6.** When they open their eyes, kiss their lips!

Rate this kiss:    Mrs.: _____/10    Mr.: _____/10

How did you feel about giving and receiving this kiss? When did you feel your sexual energy increasing, i.e. as you maintained eye contact, as you synchronized breathing or on touch?

Mrs.:

_____
_____
_____
_____

Mr.:

_____
_____
_____
_____

What variations of this tantric kiss would you like to try?

Mr.:

_____
_____
_____
_____

Mrs.:

_____
_____
_____
_____

# Red Light, Green Light

Kissing can get very intense; when things start to build in intensity, stop! This helps to bring your focus back to the present (foreplay) moment.

Stop when you want to send a message to your partner that you are enjoying yourself in the moment and don't want it to move too fast. To try this technique, choose a partner to be the "conductor" who determines when to stop. Then switch roles, so you both get a chance to control the pace.

**Play 1.** Kiss passionately, and continue until you feel things getting intense.

**Play 2.** Stop! Look at your partner's lips, breathe deeply, smile, moan, say something sexy, etc. Only start kissing again when you feel ready.

Rate this kiss:    Mrs.: _____/10    Mr.: _____/10

Does the stop and go kiss increase the intensity of the kiss for you, and if so, why?

Mrs.:

_____

_____

_____

_____

Mr.:

_____

_____

_____

_____

What variations or combinations would you like to try?

Mr.:

_____

_____

_____

_____

Mrs.:

_____

_____

_____

_____

## Playful Lips

Bring a little laughter to your make-out sessions. Take turns trying something unexpected before or during a kiss, such as:

- Ducking away when your spouse leans in for a kiss, and smiling mischievously. Do this a few times for a little game of cat-and-mouse... it's fun to be caught!

- Nibbling on your partner's lips slowly and sensually.

- While kissing in the shower, splash a little water onto your spouse's body to add excitement.

- Put a piece of fruit in your mouth, and ask your partner to take a bite. Or, rub a favorite piece of fruit over your partner's lips before you kiss them for an extra delicious taste.

- Use your imagination and invent your very own Signature Honeymoon Kiss! It can be as silly and fun as you want. Describe it here: _____

Rate these kisses:     Mrs.: _____/10     Mr.: _____/10

How did you feel about these kisses? What did you like the most, and how did you like adding playfulness?

Mrs.:

_____
_____
_____
_____

Mr.:

_____
_____
_____
_____

What other ways would you like to try to add more playfulness to your kissing foreplay?

Mr.:

_____

_____

_____

_____

Mrs.:

_____

_____

_____

_____

## Wandering Hands

A passionate kiss doesn't just have to involve your lips. Try these techniques, and you might find yourselves getting carried away (but not too much—we are still in the foreplay section!). Don't forget to take turns leading and kiss your spouse passionately throughout or after each movement below.

- Bring your hands up to your partner's face and place them on each cheek.

- Run your fingertips lightly down the front of your spouse's chest and belly—stop at the beltline!

- Wrap one arm around your partner's lower back, and place your other hand on the back of their neck. Gently pull them toward you using both hands to connect your bodies and deepen the kiss.

- Cup one butt cheek (or both!), and knead your fingers softly in a slow massage.

- Brush your hand against your spouse's inner thigh; trace small circles with your fingertips starting above the knee and progressing up the thigh, getting close to their sweet spot without actually touching it!

Rate this kiss:    Mr.: _____/10       Mrs.: _____/10

How did you feel about this kiss? Where did you like to be touched the most while kissing?

Mrs.:

_____

_____

_____

_____

Mr.:

_____

_____

_____

_____

What variations or other combinations would you like to try?

Mr.:

_____

_____

_____

_____

Mrs.:

_____

_____

_____

_____

## Tongue Games

Imagining your partner's lips and tongue on other areas of your body can be electrifying. Try these techniques on each other while you imagine them being performed on your sweet spots. Close your eyes, or keep them locked on each other—whichever is more intense for you!

- **Finger Fellatio for Him:** Make your mouth into an O shape, and slide your mouth over his index (first) finger until you reach the knuckle. With your lips locked tightly to his finger, slowly pull your lips back up to the top of his finger, and swirl your tongue across the finger pad. Next, pull his finger deep into your mouth, create a medium strong sucking action to the tip of his finger, flick your tongue, and ride back up while sucking just a little stronger this time. Repeat on different fingers. Practicing this on your own finger ahead of time will help. Sensually ask him if he would enjoy this on his penis later.

- **Finger Cunnilingus for Her:** Take the pad of her finger against your lips horizontally, and suck it against the inside of your lips. Trace a gentle circle with the point of your tongue against her finger pad, then flick the point of your tongue rapidly up and down against her finger pad. With your sexiest smile, ask her if she might also enjoy this on her clitoris later.

Rate this kiss:　　Mrs.: _____/10　　Mr.: _____/10

How did you feel about these anticipation kisses?

Mrs.:

_____
_____
_____
_____

Mr.:

_____
_____
_____
_____

What variations or combinations would you like to try?

Mr.:

_____
_____
_____
_____

Mrs.:

_____
_____
_____
_____

## Take Me Now

It can be easy to get carried away in this style of kissing, so make sure you have both discussed your boundaries and safe words before  proceeding. Questions to ask each other after reading or hearing this section might include:

- Are you ok with being pinned against a wall or bed?

- Are you ok with your hair being tugged?

- What safe words should we use if things get too intense?

- How should we let each other know that we want to stop if we are unable to speak?

**Play 1.** Choose one partner to be the dominant one (You can switch after!). The dominant partner should wait in a room until the nondominant partner enters.

*The following steps are written for and from the perspective of the dominant partner.*

**Play 2.** When your spouse enters the room, grab their shoulders firmly and guide them back up against a wall.

**Play 3.** Guide their hands above their head, and hold both against the wall with one of yours. With their hands pinned up, place your other hand on one side of their face and nibble and suck on their neck.

**Play 4.** Release their hands from above their head. Put your hands on their lower back, and pull them toward you until your bodies are pressing together tightly.

**Play 5.** Kiss them passionately.

**Play 6**. Run one hand through their hair—if they have given you permission (in advance), grab a section of hair, and gently tug it a few times.

**Play 7.** Free a hand, cup their chin in it, and pull away to look at their eyes. Hold an intense gaze for five seconds before you release their chin. As you pull away, whisper "wow" or breathe heavily to show your partner how much one simple, intense kiss can really fire you up.

**Play 8.** Take it to the bedroom, or check with your spouse to see if they would like to switch roles and play again.

Rate this kiss:     Mrs.: _____/10     Mr.: _____/10

How did you feel about this kiss? If you enjoyed it, where and when would you like to give or receive this kind of assertive kissing? For example, after work as you walk in the door? In public?

Mrs.:

_____
_____
_____
_____

Mr.:

_____
_____
_____
_____

What variations or combinations would you like to try?

Mr.:

_____
_____
_____
_____

Mrs.:

_____
_____
_____
_____

Did you prefer to be the dominant partner or the follower, and why?

Mrs.:

_____
_____
_____
_____

Mr.:

_____
_____
_____
_____

Continue to explore kissing with your partner on a regular basis. You can use kissing as a way to connect with your partner, tease, and build anticipation, and get them thinking of the other amazing things you can do with your mouth. Kiss just to acknowledge your love, or kiss as foreplay to more intimate activities—just kiss, and kiss frequently!

## Planning Plays: Your Sexual Blueprint

Your body has many erogenous zones just begging to be given unwavering attention! An erogenous zone is an area of the human body with heightened sensitivity that may produce a sexual response when stimulated. For most people, the genitals and breasts are the obvious zones and are the ones most often stimulated. But many people have heightened sensitivity in other areas of their body, including ears, nape of the neck, below the navel, back of the knee and the inner thigh to name a few. Stimulating these other zones can be excellent physical foreplay and definitely worth exploring further. In the 2008 Global Better Sex Survey, 90 percent of the women surveyed and 92 percent of the men surveyed said physical foreplay was important to their overall sexual experience. Those are percentages you just can't ignore and foreplay can add spice to your overall sexual experiences!

Our response to and enjoyment of erogenous zone stimulation may be as unique as a fingerprint: what turns you on may put your partner to sleep or be too ticklish or uncomfortable to be enjoyable. Discovering your spouse's foreplay preferences and how they want to be stimulated will allow you to tap into an even deeper sexual connection.

The following activity will give you a sexual blueprint of those hot spots, so you can learn how your spouse loves to be touched on every inch of their body. It is important to be in just the right mood before getting started, so check with your spouse to see if you are both ready to explore. Creating this blueprint should be a relaxing process for both of you, so spritz on your favourite scent, put on soft music, dim the lights, and crank the thermostat—you're going to be naked for a while! You might consider taking a relaxing aromatherapy bath together beforehand.

You will need:

- A large poster roll or end pieces of a newspaper roll large enough to trace a body. (You can often get these at your local newspaper for free or a nominal fee.)

- Use thin style paper so it can easily roll or fold into your suitcase to bring home afterward! If you really have limited space, **use the outlines in Appendix C, page 178-179.**

- Colorful markers. (You can do this activity without markers, but making it colorful is so much more fun!)

## The Warm Up

Take turns **slowly** removing each other's clothes. Kiss or touch each area of your spouse's newly exposed skin as they strip. In other words: simmer them before you crank up the heat!

Ask your spouse to lie on their back on the paper, and trace their body outline with a marker on the paper—have fun with this! It doesn't have to be perfect. Then ask them to lie down in a separate comfortable position.

### The Legend

Create a legend on the bottom right side of the paper, and include symbols to represent actions, for example, kiss, lick, suck, nibble, soft touch, tickle, firm touch. Use your imagination to come up with the types of interactions. For example, "kiss" may be represented by an X, and "lick" may be represented by a squiggle.

You may choose to also color-code the scale (e.g. dislike is red, orgasmic is green), or just use the numbers to represent intensity.

For example, if "kiss" was represented by the symbol X:

- Green X indicates orgasmic, red X indicates dislike; or,

- Four X's indicate orgasmic, one X indicates dislike.

**Test the Actions to Create a Blueprint**
Start at the feet, and work up from the outside at each area of their body. Test each action you included in your legend, and have your spouse rate the sensation using the scale of one to four. Mark the results on the trace out paper, or blueprint, of your partner's body.

Depending on your spouse's preference, you may consider only marking interactions that they rate a three or four high. If they have a particularly negative reaction, it may be helpful to mark that as well.

Remember to test different pressures and intensities for each action.

Leave the genitals until the end, so you finish the job and don't get distracted.

Adapt this activity to make it fun and informative for each of you. Don't feel the need to include absolutely every interaction on the blueprint, but do try to explore every inch of each other's bodies! Really take the time to tease all those nerve endings. When you are finished, you will have a valuable blueprint for future reference of your partner's unique erogenous zones and exactly how they like to have those zones stimulated. This is one honeymoon souvenir you just have to keep safe and refer to again!

### Have Patience!

Important rule: No getting lucky until the job is done. The simmering foreplay that occurs during this activity will likely set you or your spouse on fire. Be patient—the prize will be that much more amazing!

### Master Your Partner's Map!

When you get home from your honeymoon, discreetly tape the blueprints up on your bedroom wall or closet, and take photos with your smartphone. Make a point to study them until you are each familiar with each other's top spots! Consider these blueprints your foreplay maps: study them, and practice stimulating these areas on your spouse with focused intention (this will be the most fun you've ever had "studying").

## Muscle Warmup: Sensual Massage for Newlyweds

Massages are more than just blissful escapes. Studies show that massages can help reduce stress-causing hormones and increase serotonin and dopamine production. In other words, massages can significantly help reduce stress and anxiety. Since stress can be one of the biggest barriers to a healthy and satisfying sex life, anything that helps reduce it is a libido booster! While on your honeymoon, learn and practice giving and receiving massages, so they become an enjoyable habit when the vacation is over. You don't have to be a massage therapist to safely give a gentle sensual massage.

Although traditional massage techniques are great, a sensual massage will help you to connect with your spouse on deeper physical and emotional levels. As you massage each other, your connection to and feelings for each other will deepen.

After receiving the sensual massages below, be sure to use the space provided to rate your feelings and take notes. These will be useful the next time you dive into a blissful sensual massage!

## The Set Up

### Massage Space

Buy or borrow a well-padded massage table if possible. No massage table? Throw a few comforters on the floor, a table, or use a bed!

### Massage Tools

- feathers or something soft like a silk scarf

- massage oil (virgin coconut oil works well) with essential oil

- candles

### Music

Play your favorite sexy, slow tunes. Have a music playlist and ensure that you will respect the golden rule of massage: always have at least one part of your body (normally a hand) in contact with your partner at all times. *Check Appendix A for my personal music playlists!*

### Lighting

Light plenty of candles, real or simulated, and place them all around the massage room. If you're using a lamp instead of candles, throw a (nonflammable) colored scarf or T-shirt over the lampshade to tone down the light and add a romantic mood.

### Massage Oil and Scent

Be sure to find out what your partner's favorite scent is before your massage session. Many people enjoy sensual, arousing scents like cinnamon, ginger, jasmine, or orange. Put a few drops of your favorite scent into your massage oil. (Remember that most massage oils, like many lubricants, are not compatible with condoms or latex toys. It can degrade the latex, so the condom is much more prone to breakage.)

### Clothing

The receiver will eventually be naked. Bonus if the massager finds something sexy to wear!

## The Simmer

**Play 1.** Make sure the massage table and oil are ready to go, and the music and lighting are just right. Run a warm bubble bath, and pour a glass of your spouse's favorite beverage.

**Play 2.** *Slowly* take off your partner's clothes while teasingly and softly running your fingers over each section of their skin as you uncover it. Kiss each uncovered section slowly and with sliding kisses, i.e. sensually drag your loose lips across their skin.

**Play 3.** Lead them lovingly into the bubble bath, serve them their favorite beverage and join them.

**Play 4.** *Slowly* give your partner a frothy full body sponge bath, and focus your entire attention on them as you gently rub bubbles onto their skin with one of your hands. Your other hand follows, making the same motion with a firmer pressure.

**Play 5.** Rinse the bubbles off, then gently dry and cover your spouse with a soft, fluffy towel, and have them lie on their stomach on the massage table.

# The Relaxation Massage

Before you move to the more sensual aspects of the massage, make sure your spouse is fully relaxed and in a state of bliss. The most important thing to remember is to TAKE YOUR TIME—really feel your connection. Be smooth and gentle, make eye contact, smile, and pay attention to your spouse's reaction to your touch.

The relaxation part of the massage should last for fifteen to twenty minutes, then it's time to get sensual. Don't massage your spouse just before bed unless you want to put them to sleep! Afternoon are often the perfect time, especially after a hectic or stressful day. Let your spouse know that you have lots of time to please them. This will help to relax you both.

## Communication

The most important part of massage is communication, so ask what your spouse would enjoy and take note of their feedback. Regularly check in to see if they are enjoying the speed, movement, and pressure level you are applying. Ask them to verbally respond or make noises (e.g. moan) when they enjoy something or not.

## The Body

When your spouse is fully relaxed and comfortable, slowly trace the outer parts of their body with your hands. You can further build anticipation by dragging a feather or other soft item along the outside of their limbs. If they like a soft tickle, follow it with light pressure from your hands.

## The Head

Using your ten fingers, press down firmly on your spouse's scalp, allowing your fingers to slide gently through their hair until your palm is flat against their head and your fingers are spread far apart. Then slowly massage their scalp with your fingers in small circles. They will be putty in your hands!

## The Sensual Body Massage

Ask your partner to lie on their stomach and run feathers or feather-light fingers down the total length of their body to prepare them for a deeper massage.

Then, focus on making your hand and palm strokes long and firm. Run both hands along each side of their back, making sure to not touch the spine (touching the spine can cause discomfort and is unsafe). Maintain contact with their body with at least one hand at all times. Move your strokes outward to their sides the whole length of their back.

Be sure to massage their feet, and add massage oil warmed by your hands if needed. Massage them from their ankles up to their buttocks. Remember to use long, slow strokes adding warmed massage oil to their skin as you start to massage the inside of their thighs—intentionally slow down here as this is an important erogenous zone.

Warm up more massage oil, and massage around the outside of your spouse's butt to their lower back. Come down the center (stay away from the crack!). Slow down when you get to the bottom of their butt, and use slow, circular motions before moving back to the butt sides.

For extra sensations ask your spouse if you may straddle them (i.e. sit on their legs) to massage their mid to lower back. Straddling them is sensual in itself, and it allows you to lean in with more pressure. Give alternating sensual kisses while you apply medium pressure hand massage strokes.

Lightly tap the small of their back with the edge of your hands and loose fingers. This technique may stimulate a pleasurable arousing energy in them.

## The Sensual Chest Massage (Many men may like this too!)

Ask your spouse to flip over so they are lying on their back, and use plenty of massage oil.

Wives: You can usually press harder than you think, so ask your spouse their preferred pressure.

Husbands: How hard do you press on her breasts? No harder than the pressure you would use on your own scrotum, as breast tissue is as sensitive. Massage other chest areas first, and finish with the breasts and nipples — remember it is all about the tease.

**Play 1:** Start at the bottom of their belly area, and lightly massage with medium pressure in small circles using both full hands. Then bring your hands to the center of their belly, and slide them up the middle of the chest to just below the clavicle. Run your hands out and down the sides of the breasts to the belly again (repeat 3x).

Remember to add more massage oil as needed.

**Play 2:** Massage small circles with your palms on each breast just above the areola, moving up to the clavicle. This is one of the most sensual areas of the breasts, so spend a few minutes applying medium pressure. The rhythm should be slow and sensual.

**Play 3:** Gently massage circles with your full hands around each breast. Go very slowly and keep a steady rhythm for about 2 minutes.

**Play 4:** With the tip of your fingers, trace small circles just inside the areolas and with every circle make smaller and smaller circles until you are making tiny circles right on top of the nipples.

**Play 5:** Place your thumbs and fingers around each nipple, at the outside edge of each areola. Slowly and gently bring your thumbs and fingers together to squeeze the nipples, and then pull them outward. This technique may stimulate a pleasurable arousal.

**Play 6:** Slowly and sensually kiss and suck each nipple, and be aware of your spouse's desired pressure. Remember to add eye contact from time to time to intensify your connection.

Which parts of this massage did you enjoy? Which parts (if any!) did you not enjoy?

With soft hands, slowly brush your hands from the outside of each breast to the top of each thigh. Then massage slowly with a hand on each leg in a circular motion from each knee to the top of each thigh. When you get close to the inner thigh, slow down, and gaze into their eyes with loving intention. If your partner can't stand the teasing any longer, don't leave your spouse frustrated! Now is the time to give yourself fully to your partner.

Which parts of this massage did you enjoy? Which parts (if any!) did you not enjoy?

Mr.:

_____

_____

_____

_____

Mrs.:

_____

_____

_____

_____

Referring to the above notes in the future will not only bring back great sentimental memories, it will also serve as an ongoing reference to improve your massage techniques. Never stop learning how to massage to better pleasure each other!

## Foreplay Recap

Foreplay is equally important to women and men—taking your time to get warmed up makes your sexual experiences that much more intense! In this section, you learned:

- You can build anticipation by talking about sex, and it can be just as exciting as other types of foreplay.

- You can really get the juices going by kissing, an amazing form of intimacy.

- Your spouse has unique erogenous zones that can make them crazy with desire.

- Massage isn't just for getting out knots. It can be an erotic experience in itself!

SEX

Your guide to "scoring" the best romantic honeymoon ever!

# SEX

Whether or not you made love on your wedding night (if you didn't, you're not alone!), your honeymoon is the perfect opportunity to connect deeply on an intimate level with your new spouse. Getting away from it all is the best time to really get into it! After the stress of planning the wedding and the emotional roller coaster of the day itself, your honeymoon is a time to relax, de-stress, and explore each other's minds and bodies without the pressure or interference of daily life.

Don't put too much pressure on yourselves, however, to make your honeymoon sex the best of your life. It's ok if you don't have wild, animalistic sex all day every day of your honeymoon (but it's ok if you do!). There is no need to go into your honeymoon with unrealistic expectations or anxieties. Give yourself permission to just relax and have fun, and you might find that sex comes more naturally.

If you're anxious to make things as hot as possible on your honeymoon, have a discussion before your trip. What do you both want your honeymoon to look like? If you both value having lots of intimate time together, try not to fill up your schedules with sightseeing and adventure tours as you'll need the extra time and energy! Peruse some of the activities in this book, talk about them, and take note of the indoor activities that pique your interest.

How can this Playbook help? The games and activities in this section are designed to ignite your raw sexual instincts! Fanning the flames of your sexual relationship on your honeymoon is a great way to set the stage for a hot and connected marriage for years to come and create lasting and satisfying memories.

This section includes:

- The Pleasure Anatomy Plays

- Sexy Games

## Know Your Game: The Pleasure Anatomy Plays

Many couples make the mistake of focusing in on only the most obvious parts of their partner's genitals. However, every part can be used to heighten pleasure. Learning exactly what to do will take your sexual experiences to the next level on your honeymoon, and for years to come. Taking the time to ask your spouse for feedback will make you a confident lover—and confidence is sexy!

In this section, you will go through a series of steps (plays) designed to focus your attention on each area of your spouse's genitals. At the end of each activity, take down general notes. You can do this at the end of the entire activity if you are really getting into the moment. Having an accurate record will not only help you to remember what is important to do again, but it will also serve as a souvenir of what you discovered on your honeymoon.

*"My husband and I have repeated these activities over time, and despite our many years of marriage we always discover something new."*

# THE VULVA

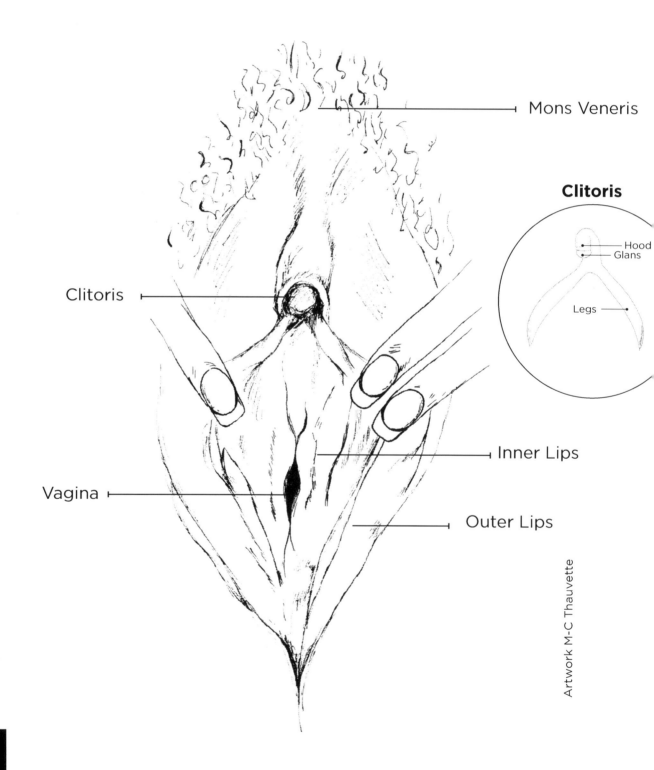

Mons Veneris

**Clitoris**

Hood
Glans

Legs

Clitoris

Inner Lips

Vagina

Outer Lips

Artwork M-C Thauvette

# THE PENIS

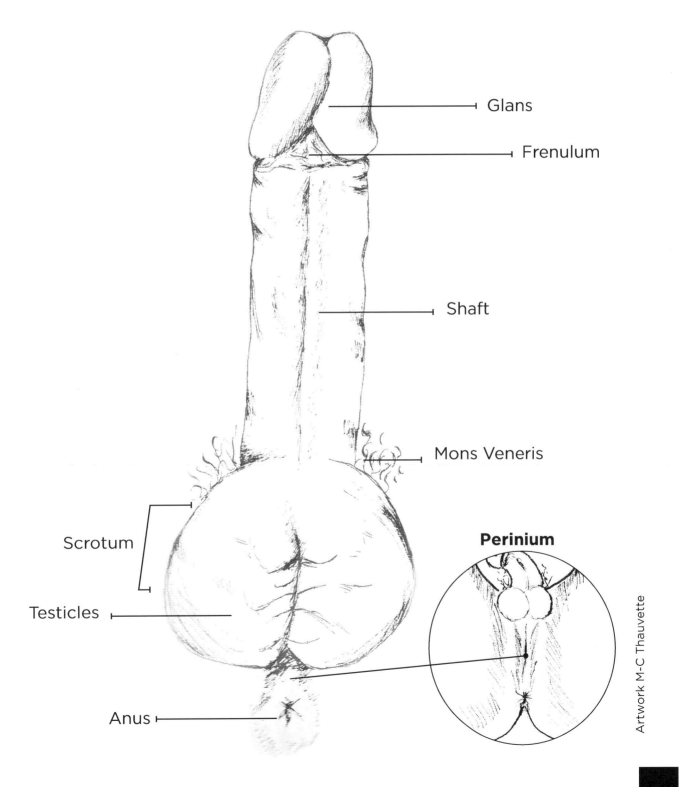

Glans

Frenulum

Shaft

Mons Veneris

**Perinium**

Scrotum

Testicles

Anus

## He's on Deck... Mastering the Vulva Pleasure Anatomy

Like any game requiring physical effort, you need to warm up first! Get both of your heart rates elevated with lots of slow and sensual kissing (pages 71-93), or give her a sensual massage (pages 102-106). When you're both warmed up, tell your wife you want to get intimate with every inch of her vulva and learn what she loves. Let her know she should let you know what feels good. If you are the playful type, give her vulva or, even better, her clitoris a cute nickname:_____.
Tell her to lay back and relax—this is all about her pleasure! And remember, practice makes perfect.

Equipment:
- Water-based lubrication or coconut oil

- A playful and fun attitude

## The Forgotten Play: Remembering the Outer Lips (Labia Majora) & Inner Lips (Labia Minora)

Although the lips are the most visible part of the vulva, they are usually neglected during lovemaking. Pay lots of attention to these ladies during foreplay! You may notice her lips are not even—this is perfectly normal, but many women are self-conscious about it. Be sure to tell your wife just how beautiful and sexy you find every part of her (and maybe especially these parts).

**Tip:** Be sure to run your fingers through her pubic hair to catch little strands, as this can be unexpectedly enjoyable for her!

Use the following delightful lip massage-stimulation sequence to find out exactly what your wife loves. Ask her to rate the sensations on a scale of 1 to 10 after you perform each "play":

**Hint:** Ladies, you may want to try this sequence yourself (minus the licking section, of course). Explore away so you can play show and tell with him later. Be confident! Studies show men love a confident woman in the bedroom. Remember to use your sexiest voice when giving him your positive directions, and lots of oral feedback (moaning counts) on what you love.

Use the following delightful lip massage-stimulation sequence to find out exactly what your wife loves. Ask her to rate her sensations on a scale of 1 to 10 after you perform each "play".

## Outer Lips
**"Let's give these girls lots of love ..."**

Ask your wife to lie down comfortably on a bed with her legs over the edge, close her eyes, and concentrate on the sensations you are about to give her. Position yourself between her legs at the end of the bed with your knees on pillows on the floor.

**Play 1.** Rub your hands together until they get comfortably warm, and place your dominant hand on top of her outer lips with your palm directly on top of the clitoral hood area. Stay there until she says she feels the warmth from your hand.
/10

**Play 2.** Continue by using your dominant hand to make slow, even gentle pressured circles. Try different pressures and directions to see what she likes.
/10

**Play 3.** Dip your thumb and index finger in water-based lube or coconut oil.

Starting at the bottom of the right outer lip, gently roll it slowly and smoothly between your fingers, and keep rolling your fingers up the lip slowly until you reach the clitoris glans area. She may enjoy your spending a little more time there as it can really tease her. Do the same with the left outer lip.
/10

**Play 4.** Gather the outer lips together by placing your index finger and thumb on each side, and bring the two sides together. Start at the bottom of the outer lips, then slide the lips together back and forth from the bottom to the top of the clitoral glans area. Spend more time near her clitoris glans area for extra teasing. For more variety try again with a rolling motion between your finger and thumb.   /10

**Play 5.** Lay four fingertips on the bottom of each of the outer lips, and press slow, firm, dime-like circles up to the clitoral glans area. Repeat several times and then stay in her clitoral area. Increase your speed and vary your pressure, and take note of what she prefers.
/10

Which steps does she want to try again and why?

Comments: _____

_____

## Inner Lips
### "Where his lips kiss your lips and more…"

**Play 1.** First open her outer lips and offer her inner lips a long lingering kiss similar to her favorite kiss on her other lips (check kissing section pages 71-93). Kissing anytime during love making can result in a deeper connection and improve your already strong bond. Be sure to ask her how she prefers to be kissed on each set of lips.
 /10

**Play 2.** Open her outer lips to expose her beautifully-shaped inner lips. She can hold them open for you if she likes for better access.

Take one of her inner lips between your lips (no teeth please!) and gently suck it. Ask her if she likes to have you flick your tongue as you are sucking. As you pull away, finish with a lingering kiss. Suck on different sides and places on her inner lips until X marks the spot of maximum pleasure. This is all about your play and discovery of her pleasure.
 /10

**Play 3.** Lick each inner lip with one steady lick from the bottom to the top.  Then try short, quick licks and flicks up each side. Ask her to let you know what she prefers and where, or just observe and note her most enjoyable moans, groans, or heavy breathing.
 /10

Which steps does she want to try again and why?


Comments: _____

_____

## He Takes the Mound: Massaging the Mons Veneris

The Latin term mons veneris means "mound of Venus" (the Roman goddess of love). The best attribute of this wonderfully rounded mass of fatty tissue lying over the pubic bones is the special real estate it occupies—the mons is just above her best friend, the clitoris. Keep that in mind while you are exploring! Ask your wife to rate each of the following "plays" on a scale of 1 to 10.

**Play 1.** Using the tips of your fingers and a little bit of your nails, softly pet her mons from top to bottom. Pick up your hand and start at the top again as if you are petting a kitten. End your "pet" on top of her clitoral area. Purrrr!

/10

Comments: _____

**Play 2.** Rub your hands together until they feel warm, and then lay one hand on top of her mons; the heel of your hand should be on the clitoral area. With even pressure make small circles with your whole palm. Keep an eye on her face and listen to her sounds to know when and how to change the pressure. Stay with the same pressure when you see intense pleasure signs.

/10

Comments: _____

# Get the Ball Rolling: Stimulating the Clitoris

Many women are unaware that their clitoris is not only the little external bundle of nerves we know and love so much, but, in fact, has "legs," that hide under the inner lips and stretch to the bottom of the vaginal entrance.

In fact, there is some discussion that the clitoris and the G-spot are not distinct organs but part of the same tissue complex—in short, the G-spot may simply be the back of the clitoris. The little clitoral nub itself can have up to eight thousand nerve endings! Try the following techniques to really make her glow. We are all different, so don't forget to ask your wife to give feedback on the following "plays".

**Play 1.** Put a soft sock or material on top of a vibrator and gently place it over various parts of her clitoris. The dulled vibrations will increase pleasurable sensations in her more gradually.
/10
Comments: _____

**Play 2.** Add more lube to your fingers, and push her mons up to expose her clitoris. Gently probe until you find a small firm stalk beneath the clitoral head—it is like a tiny little boner! Remember to be gentle as women are often very sensitive here because of the amount of nerve endings. Once you've located the clitoris, gently pinch it between your thumb and forefinger and massage it up and down, similar to how you would your penis. Be sure to ask her about her preferred pressure and speed.
/10
Comments: _____

**Play 3.** Divide and conquer! Divide her clitoris area into four quadrants (top/bottom and left/right), and gently stimulate each quadrant with a well-lubed finger or two in a slow circular motion until she responds. Continue to experiment with gentle pressures and speeds on the top of her clitoral hood. Note her preferences.

Note: Where and how does she prefer her clitoris stimulated?
/10
Comments: _____

## Through the Five Hole: Pleasuring the Vagina

**Play 1.** Enter her vagina with a finger or sex toy, but be sure she is very stimulated. If you've been playing along, she should be! Arousal will not only cause her to secrete more lubrication but also cause her vaginal opening to double in diameter. Stimulate her clitoris at the same time to help bring her to orgasm. Note that not many women can orgasm from vaginal stimulation alone.

**Play 2.** Find her G-spot. It is located two knuckles in and up on the belly side of her vagina. If she is well stimulated, you should find a quarter-sized, sponge-like section: that is it! Use your middle finger to make steady come-hither motions on it while also stimulating her clitoris with another finger.
/10
Comments: _____

## She's on Deck... Mastering His Penis Pleasure Anatomy

Before you start, make sure to put on something you feel sexy in. Men are visual creatures, and if you feel sexy and confident your husband will notice! Highlight your most seductive features. When you feel ready, tell him to lie back and relax—this is all about his pleasure. Enjoy the feeling of the two of you growing close and more excited with every new experience! After you have performed each activity below, have your spouse rate it on a scale of 1 to 10. To start, bring him to the edge of a bed with his legs off the edge, put pillows under your knees, and open his legs. Before you begin, honor your husband's most important pleasure center, his penis, by giving it a pet name: _____.

## Balls in Play: Handling the Testicles

There are plenty of nerve endings in his family jewels, but most men agree that their "Bojangles" are too often neglected during sex play. Don't be afraid to explore this pleasure center, but this area is sensitive, so experiment with gentle play. During these activities, check with your husband regularly to make sure he's enjoying himself. Now let's get the "balls" rolling!

**Play 1.** Start with his pants or underwear ON. Press gentle circles over his whole scrotum area with your fingertips. Gently move your fingertips bottom to top and back down his scrotum. Tease him by first pressing the centre of his scrotum up to the top of his glans with a few fingers, then press it back down again. Smile at him seductively while you do this! Then lean in, open your mouth, press your lips on to his scrotum area, and blow some steamy, hot air through his underwear to really heat things up.

/10

Comments: _____

**Play 2.** Now that you have sufficiently warmed him up, slowly and confidently take his pants and underwear off. If you are feeling particularly confident, release your inner wild woman and use your teeth to remove them! Make eye contact as much as you can, especially while using your teeth, as this will deepen your love-making connection.

/10

Comments: _____

**Play 3.** Load up both hands with lots of lube, put one hand under his scrotum and the other hand on top. With the upper hand, gently make slow massage circles over his balls. To tease him further feather your fingers over the length of his shaft.

/10

Comments: _____

**Play 4.** Experiment with pleasuring his testicles using different motions: cup them, pet them, kiss them, lightly roll them, lick them, bring them into your mouth and gently suck them, scratch them (gently!). Just remember that the pressure should always be very light unless he says otherwise, and pay attention to his reactions. /10

Comments: _____

**Play 5.** Cup the top of his sack with your non-dominant hand then gently lay the fingers of your dominant hand underneath. Starting with the baby finger in your dominant hand, roll each finger up to your index finger in a come-hither movement and repeat. Pay attention to what pressure and timing he prefers.

/10

Comments: _____

**Play 6.** Once you know he is thoroughly excited, try gently pulling his sack away from his body. You can also try a little tug to the left and right. This works during oral sex and intercourse to heighten his sensations—but normally only when he's worked up!
/10
Comments: _____

## She Takes the Mound: Experimenting with the Mons Pubis

The mons is located on the pubic bone where there is usually hair growth. This section includes the lower belly, which is also an underappreciated erogenous zone for many men.

**Play 1.** Start by putting lots of lube on your hands. Place one hand on his mons and the other on his perinium, forming a circle around his penis and balls. Make slow massage circles, reverse your direction, then "accidently" ride one hand up his shaft. DON'T continue there even if he begs you; there is a lot more experimenting to go.
/10
Comments: _____

**Play 2.** Gently take the base of his penis in your hand, and flick it onto his mons and lower belly. Experiment with speed—most men like quick firm flicks. This will help increase blood flow to his penis, and doing it during foreplay or sex will often help wake him back up and stand at attention for you.
/10
Comments: _____

*"At one time or another, a man's penis will likely return to being flaccid during lovemaking. If this happens, it's no big deal. Just keep playing! Give it some love! I say flick it, kiss it, lick it, and figure out what he loves, so he can come out to play with you again. It's all part of the fun!"*

## The Hidden Play: Remembering the Perineum

The perineum is the part of the body between your husband's scrotum and anus. It is often called a man's pleasure button. Why? Firstly, there are a lot of nerve endings in that area. Secondly, it is very close to the prostate, considered to be a man's G-spot.

**Play 1.** With lots of lubrication, firmly press your index and middle fingers in the little groove area (check illustration on page 113). Try every direction: up and down, side to side, and around this dime-sized area. Check with him to see how much pressure he likes. This massage may heighten arousal sensations in some men. For others, the massage will simply be pleasurable.
/10
Comments: _____

**Play 2.** You each have a role to play during this step.

**For the groom:**
First of all, focus on relaxing every muscle in your body, especially the lower body, while she is pleasing you. Really absorb the sensations, and feel the love your wife is giving you.

**For the bride:**
Give him a big smile, and be sure to hold eye contact for a couple of seconds. His knowing you are enjoying yourself is very important to his pleasure. Never forget that the biggest sexual organ is between the ears.

Put your non-dominant hand palm up under his family jewels, with your palm on his perineum. Put your thumb on one side and your other fingers on the other side of his package. Then place your dominant hand palm down over his mons. Put circular pressure with your lower palm on the perineum area, and medium pressure with your upper palm on his mons. While you keep that circular motion going, lean in and suck gently and then firmly on his penis.

/10

Comments: _____

*"Men surveyed said that they especially loved it when their wives delivered these moves with intensity and passion. Men got very excited when their lovers were really into it. Having both of their partner's hands on their erogenous zones while receiving oral pleasure made them feel intensely stimulated. They said that this technique was so different from what they had felt before, and the newness of it was so exciting, they begged to have their lovers do it again!"*

# High-Sticking: Stroking the Shaft

The shaft has a really important job! It's the most important blood pumping tool on a man's pleasure anatomy. However, this pleasure stick does not have as many pleasure nerve endings as other parts of his anatomy. Most of his sexual pleasure nerves are located just below his glans, or head.

The most important part of playing with the shaft (actually, with any part of the pleasure anatomy!) is LUBE. This is something you want to pay attention to while on your honeymoon. Without enough lube, both of you can go raw in a hurry, and that's a BIG NO-NO at this special time.

**Play 1.** Introduce a "sleeve" or "stroker" toy; there are many varieties available. Men are usually pleasantly surprised by how much they love the way it hugs their shaft. Always check with your husband about how much pressure he prefers. Some men need a lot of pressure, and they usually prefer it at the top of the shaft. This can be tough to achieve with penetration, so let the sleeve toy do most of the work! Remember to add a lot of water-based lubricant on the sleeve.
/10
Comments: _____

**Play 2.** Ride the BOOBS! Most men would say that the boobs and shaft are meant to meet more often! Place your chest on top of his shaft, surround it with your breasts, pushing them in from the outside, and let him ride your "boob crack" up and down, or jiggle your boobs yourself. Don't worry about how big your "boob crack" is; men just love the visual.
/10
Comments: _____

**Play 3.** Let your husband pleasure himself while you watch, but don't let him come yet! Observing him will help you notice a lot of details that you can mimic later. Is his grip low or high on the shaft? Is his rhythm fast, slow or both? Is he varying the motion?

/10

Comments: _____

**Play 4.** Using both hands, and again, lots of lube, give a slippery twist up and down his shaft. Vary the speed and pressure of your twists, and observe what your husband prefers.

/10

Comments: _____

# Double Header: Two Ways to Play with the Glans

The glans, or head, of the penis is where the action is. This is where most of his pleasure nerves are, so make sure to really give them some love!

**Play 1.** Using lots of lube, place your non-dominant hand underneath his scrotum. Put the palm of your dominant hand on top of his glans, and experiment to see just what he likes: try making circles, going back and forth, starting slow and increasing your speed, then vary your speed. Enjoy that stick shift!

/10

Comments: _____

*"Use a sleeve that has a hole at the top, as this allows you to pleasure him orally at the same time so he will have the best of both worlds."*

**Play 2.** Use your mouth! Using lubed hands, make a gentle twisting motion on his shaft and then teasingly press your lips to his glans. Be sure to keep your teeth out of the way! While your mouth works its magic, make sure your hands stay attached to his shaft at all times. Use your lips and mouth to create suction on the upstroke.

/10

Comments: _____

# Scoring Extra Points: The Frenulum and Mouth Play

The frenulum is located right under the glans on the underside of the penis shaft (see page 113). This is often the most arousing spot on a man's penis. Paying special attention to it will keep your husband hopped up on pleasure.

**Play 1.** Try licking the frenulum up and down, side-to-side, and then vary the pressure and speed of your tongue to find his sweet spot.
/10
Comments: _____

**Play 2.** If he can handle a little more sensation, try slightly opening your mouth and pressing your lips down firmly on the frenulum. Give it a little sucking action while quickly moving your tongue back and forth on his glans.
/10
Comments: _____

Remember to take notes on his preferences, and refer to them regularly as you make them all a part of your repertoire. This will be a great souvenir of your honeymoon lovemaking!

## The Playoffs: Sexy Games

Sex doesn't have to follow a set formula. Get your adrenaline pumping, and boost your excitement levels through the roof with some high energy sex games! Some couples maintain that make-up sex has been the best lovemaking they have ever had. Why? When we are excited by one stimulus such as an argument, we are likely to be easily excited by another one such as sexual touching. This is called transfer of arousal.

Transfer of arousal doesn't just happen from negative stimuli like a fight—it can happen from positive stimuli too. Getting your heart rates pumping with activities can result in heightened sexual arousal. So, have fun and enjoy the results of these adrenaline pumping sex games!

But first, make sure you discuss each other's boundaries in detail. Check in with your partner in advance to confirm what you are okay with exploring, and what you would rather not give consent to. Establish a safe word, so you can both be comfortable knowing that there is a way to stop play if one person is uncomfortable. You can talk and decide after you stop if and how to proceed further. Safe words can be any word (or a combination of words) that you would be unlikely to use during sex or play. Choosing a word that has nothing to do with lovemaking is the best strategy to avoid confusion. Discussing your boundaries and establishing a safe word will put both of you at ease.

The games included in this section are:

- Kissing Cards

- The Newlywed Game with a Twist

- Slippery Wrestling

- Indoor or Outdoor Water FIGHT

- Hide and Strip

- Hide and Ice

- Nerf or Sock War

- Strip Tickle Fight

- One Step Closer

- Fast Sex

# Kissing Cards

## Equipment and Supplies

- Deck of cards

- 1 spoon

## Object of the Game

To kiss and be kissed!

## How to Play

- Shuffle a deck of cards, and divide the pack in half. Each of you take a pile.

- Place the spoon exactly halfway between you.

- Each of you lays down a card from your pile beside the spoon at the same time.

- When you both lay down cards of the same suit, each of you tries to grab the spoon.

- Whoever grabs the spoon first is the winner of that round and gets to receive a special kiss. Start at kiss #1 below, and progress to receive the next kiss every time you win. The first person to receive all ten kisses wins!

**Kisses**

1. Slowly and seductively kiss their bottom lip.
2. Slowly and seductively kiss their top lip.
3. Teasingly kiss their neck.
4. Kiss while you are holding on to both their cheeks.
5. Kiss while you play with their hair.
6. Kiss while both hands are on their bum.
7. Kiss while one hand is on their chest and the other is on their thigh.
8. Kiss while one hand is on their thigh and one hand is on their favorite erogenous zone.
9. Press them against a wall and sensually kiss them.
10. Have the lighter partner straddle (sit on top of) the other partner while kissing.

**Rate the game**

Mrs.:　　　/10
Mr.:　　　/10

**After You're Finished**

Answer the following questions by filling in the blanks below. Be specific! For example, "I loved kiss #5 because I love having my hair played with!"

Which kiss was the most romantic?

Mrs.:

_____
_____
_____
_____

Mr.:

_____
_____
_____
_____

Which kiss turned you on the most?

Mr.:

_____
_____
_____
_____

Mrs.:

_____
_____
_____
_____

# The Newlywed Game with a Twist!

## Equipment and Supplies
- Paper, cut into small sections

- Two pens

- Two hats or creative containers

- Soft neckties or scarves

## Object of the Game
Learn more about your partner in a sexy way.

## How to Play
- Each of you writes down ten trivia-style questions about yourself on the sections of paper.

- Put the questions into different hats or containers (or keep them in separate piles).

- Flip a coin to see who gets to ask questions first.

- The winner pulls a question out of their hat, and asks their partner.

- If your partner gets the answer wrong, tie one of their wrists or ankles to a bed, to their body, to your body, etc. Then pull and ask the next question. Keep tying them up for wrong answers!

- Once all the questions are answered (or they are completely tied up) have your way with them!

- Switch partners so they ask their set of questions.

**Rate the game**

Mrs.:          /10

Mr.:          /10

**After You're Finished**

Answer the following questions by filling in the blanks below.
Be specific!

What interesting thing did you learn about your spouse?

Mrs.:

_____
_____
_____
_____

Mr.:

_____
_____
_____
_____

How did being tied up (or having your partner tied up) make you feel?

Mr.:

_____
_____
_____
_____

Mrs.:

_____
_____
_____

# Slippery Wrestling

**Equipment and Supplies:**

- Plastic sheet (a shower curtain works!)

- Oil (coconut oil works well)

- Underwear you are ok with throwing away afterwards

- Nontoxic, nonstaining foam or paint

**Object of the Game**

Get your partner's underwear off first!

**How to Play**

Put the plastic sheet on a bed or floor to protect it from the oil. Slather oil on each other, so you are both nice and slippery. Wrestle until someone gets the other person's underwear off! You can find your partner's most ticklish spot and attack it while wrestling.

**Too easy? Try these variations**

- One or both of you cannot use one or both of their hands.

- One or both of you must stay on your knees.

- One partner must close their eyes.

**Rate the game**

Mrs.:        /10

Mr.:        /10

**After You're Finished**

Answer the following questions by filling in the blanks below. Be specific!

What part of the game, and/or which variation turned you on the most?

Mr.:

_____

_____

_____

_____

Mrs.:

_____

_____

_____

_____

# Indoor or Outdoor Water FIGHT!

## Equipment and Supplies

- Two loaded water guns
- A note pad and pen
- Two white T-shirts

## Object of the Game

Get each other nice and wet and enjoy the view!

## How to Play

- Send your partner out of the room to get ice or to shower, or wait until they leave your room temporarily.

- When they are gone, place a note (see example below), white T-shirt, and a water gun in an easily visible place.

- Put on the other white T-shirt, take your loaded water gun, and hide yourself well!

- When your partner sees the note and the gun, instruct them to put on their t-shirt and let the games begin!

*The note could say...*

Dear husband/wife,
Your gun is loaded, but so is mine. As of now, you are officially UNDER ATTACK! Come find me, and let the best man/woman win! "Best" may mean best shot, best looking when wet, or whatever you decide.

*"My husband and I had an absolute blast playing this game. We were laughing so hard, I called time out for a bathroom break! He loved the wet white T-shirt look, and I couldn't get over how quickly we needed to take this game outside. When outside, we kept it going until we started rolling in the grass and couldn't resist each other any longer. It was some of the best sex we'd ever had."*

**Rate the game**

Mrs.:        /10

Mr.:        /10

**After You're Finished**

Answer the following questions by filling in the blanks below.
Be specific!

How did this game turn you on?

Mrs.:

_____

_____

_____

_____

Mr.:

_____

_____

_____

_____

# Hide and Strip!

**Equipment and Supplies**

- Five to ten articles of clothing for each of you to put on together

- A timer device to make a loud sound (your cell phone or a kitchen timer works)

- A space with lots of hiding places

- Sexy music

**Object of the Game**

Get your spouse naked!

**How to Play**

- Flip a coin to decide who wins (they will hide first).

- The loser of the coin toss will close their eyes, face a wall, and slowly count to twenty out loud while their spouse hides. (If your space is particularly big, you may need more time to hide.)

- After the twenty count is done, set the timer for thirty seconds (or one minute if the space is large) and try to find your hidden partner before time runs out!

- If you find your spouse before the timer goes off, they must strip off one article of clothing. If you don't they get to keep their clothing on.

- Take turns counting and hiding, and continue until someone is completely naked!

*Variation: Hide and Dominate!*

If you find them before the timer goes off, they become your sexual slave for one minute! (Or, if you prefer giving pleasure, you can ask to become their sexual slave for one minute!)

**Rate the game**
Mrs.:          /10
Mr.:          /10

**After You're Finished**
Answer the following questions by filling in the blanks below.
Be specific!

How did this game, or a variation, turn you on?

Mr.:

_____

_____

_____

_____

Mrs.:

_____

_____

_____

_____

# Hide and Ice!

## Equipment and Supplies

- Two blindfolds

- Big ice cubes in a bucket

- A timer device (cell phone works)

- Lingerie for her and sexy underwear for him

- A small space (1 or 2 rooms)

## Object of the Game

Get hot while you get cold!

## How to Play

- Flip a coin to decide who will count first (winner decides).

- The counter puts on a blindfold, faces a wall, and counts to twenty out loud while their partner quietly hides (but not too far away). The hiding partner also puts on a blindfold once they have hidden.

- The counter sets the timer for thirty seconds, and grabs a nearby ice cube from the bucket. They then try to find their hidden partner before time runs out!

- If the counter finds their partner before the timer goes off, they get to rub the ice cube on their partner's body slowly and seductively (keep your blindfolds on—no peeking!), or share an icy kiss. They may alternatively slip the ice cube just under the bra or underwear line of their spouse for a sexy tease.

- Switch roles, and continue until you both can't take the cold, the teasing, or both!

## Variation

The person who is found can choose what they desire to be done with the ice cube.

## Rate the game

Mrs.:        /10

Mr.:        /10

## After You're Finished

Answer the following questions by filling in the blanks below.
Be specific!

How did the ice make you feel?

Mr.:

_____

_____

_____

_____

Mrs.:

_____

_____

_____

_____

# Nerf® or Sock War

### Equipment and Supplies

- One Nerf® gun and ammo, or clean socks rolled up in a ball

- Sexy underwear or lingerie for her and cute underwear for him

### Object of the Game
Hit the bulls-eye.

### How to Play

- Flip a coin to see who starts (shooter).

- The loser of the coin toss has to stand spread eagled against a wall with their back to their partner to become the target.

- The shooter stands behind a predetermined line (e.g. 15 ft away).

- The shooter shoots the nerf, or throws a sock. If they hit their partner's body, they must kiss, lick, or nibble that spot (The target cannot move while they do this).

- If the shooter gets three out of three shots on their spouse's body, their spouse must turn around, and the shooter gets three more shots (and kisses, etc. when they hit a target)!

- If and when the shooter misses one of the first three shots, they must change places with their partner and they become the target.

### Variation
The target chooses whether to get a kiss, lick, or nibble when and where they are hit.

**Rate the game**

Mrs.:          /10

Mr.:          /10

**After You're Finished**

Answer the following questions by filling in the blanks below.
Be specific!

Did you enjoy shooting your spouse or being shot by the Nerf®
or sock?

Mr.:

_____

_____

_____

_____

Mrs.:

_____

_____

_____

_____

# Strip Tickle Fight

## Equipment and Supplies

- Strip music (download a favourite playlist or album from your music provider; it will serve you well for repeat plays!)

- Each of you dresses in five articles of clothing

## Object of the Game

Get laughing!

## How to Play

Note: tickle fight only when you are both neither hungry nor tired as you need to be positive and gentle to each other!

- Start tickling each other—slowly at first. Feel free to get excited, run away, and chase one another!

- Whichever partner can't take it first uses the safe "stop" word and must remove an article of clothing seductively while music plays—the other partner gets to choose which one! Get into the strip tease—channel your inner stripper.

- If you feel like it, continue to strip for your partner, and see where it leads. If not, do more rounds of tickle fighting!

**Rate the game**

Mrs.:　　　/10

Mr.:　　　/10

**After You're Finished**

Answer the following questions by filling in the blanks below.
Be specific!

Did you enjoy being tickled? Did you most enjoy stripping or watching your partner strip?

Mrs.:

_____

_____

_____

_____

Mr.:

_____

_____

_____

_____

# One Step Closer

**Equipment and Supplies**

- Your most seductive underwear or lingerie (both of you)

- Each of you prepares five to ten trivia questions about yourself and put them in separate piles

**Object of the game**

Learn about your spouse.

**How to Play**

- Flip a coin to determine who asks questions first.

- The flipped coin loser (Asker) stands at a door with their back to the room while their partner (Walker) stands across the room.

- Asker then pulls a question from their pile and asks the Walker.

- For each answer guessed correctly, Walker progresses two steps forward toward the Asker.

- For each question guessed incorrectly, the Walker takes one step backward.

- When the Asker thinks the Walker is close enough, instead of asking their next question, they may spin around quickly and yell, "No more questions!" while trying to catch the Walker.

- If the Asker touches the Walker before they reach the other side of the room, the Asker may have their way with the Walker! If the Walker reaches the other side before they are caught, switch roles and start over.

**Rate the game**
Mrs.:          /10
Mr.:           /10

**After You're Finished**
Answer the following questions by filling in the blanks below. Be specific!

What did you learn about your spouse?

Mr.:

_____
_____
_____
_____

Mrs.:

_____
_____
_____
_____

# Fast Sex

## Equipment and Supplies

- Timer (cell phone works)

## Object of the Game

Have a quickie!

## How to Play

- Use some of the other games in this section as foreplay.

- When both of you are revved up and ready to go, pick a comfortable spot, turn on the timer for about one minute and start having fast sex!

- When the timer runs out, run to a new location, restart the timer, and continue your fast sex!

- Don't only go to obvious spots: try some new ones like in the closets and on various furniture.

- Stopping to switch locations will get harder and harder to do!

## Rate the game

Mrs.:       /10

Mr.:       /10

## After You're Finished

Answer the following questions by filling in the blanks below. Be specific!

What was your favorite location?

Mrs.:

_____

_____

_____

_____

Mr.:

_____

_____

_____

_____

## Summary

The Bride's Scoreboard on which sex games she preferred:
1. _____
2. _____
3. _____
4. _____
5. _____

The Groom's Scoreboard on which sex games he preferred:
1. _____
2. _____
3. _____
4. _____
5. _____

## Sex Recap

Deep physical intimacy strengthens and helps sustain long-term relationships. In this section, you learned:

- Exactly how your spouse loves their sexual anatomy to be handled.

- New and exciting games to spice up your sexual play!

# FINAL THOUGHTS

Your guide to "scoring" the best romantic honeymoon ever!

# FINAL THOUGHTS

I hope that this Playbook has helped (or will help!) your honeymoon to be the most memorable trip of your life. Developing and keeping sexually engaging energy between you long after your honeymoon is over is crucial to a happy and long-lasting marriage. If you've written in the pages of this Playbook, keep your notes handy to draw upon for continuing inspiration when romance, foreplay, and sex start to become routine. Take what you've learned and practice it regularly with your new spouse, and don't be afraid to keep experimenting and learning! As the years go on, repeat and refine the activities in this book, and discover new ones. You may be surprised how much you can still learn about your spouse, ten or even fifty years after your honeymoon is over. Your bodies and tastes will change over time, so you will want to reread and redo this Playbook on your second honeymoon and beyond!

Feeling a solid sense of affirmation and love from your spouse, and returning these, is crucial to an enduring relationship. Affection and deep attachment are built on the everyday interactions and experiences you share as a couple. Loyalty and devotion are built in large part from the intimate activities that nurture your spousal relationship.

If you need help along the way, I am just a quick e-mail away at mc@relationshipbliss.ca. Wishing the two of you a blissfully romantic, playful and sensual long & happily married life together.

With Love,

*MC Thauvette*

# APPENDIX A

## Performance Enhancers: Sex Toys

Sex toys are a great way to add some excitement and variety to your sex life.

*"My husband and I have been together for twenty years, and our love-making continues to be fun and alive. One of the reasons is because we include sex toys!"*

Sex toys can be used individually or together during your lovemaking. There is a staggering variety of choices available, and finding toys that you enjoy is half the fun!

## Toys to Try

- **For her:** Bullets, or minivibrators, like the Touch and Tango are perfect first sex toys. Their small size make them easy to reach down and position in the clitoral area during most sexual positions. If it feels too strong, try holding a piece of soft material or a sock over it to dull the vibrations.

- **For him:** An open sleeve toy that fits over his penis can make fellatio even more pleasurable for him and easier for you. Sleeves are typically made of soft, flexible material that grips the shaft of the penis and easily slide up and down. Use lots of water-based lube for more comfort!

- **For both:** U-shaped vibrators such as the "We-Vibe Unite" provide powerful vibration that can be pleasurable for both of you. The smaller arm of the U goes inside her and stimulates her G-spot. It is small enough to be used during penetration, yet he can feel the vibrations from the larger arm. It will even stimulate her clitoris and his balls against his shaft.

## Using Toys with Lube

Using the correct lubrication with your sex toys is critical to your health and maintaining the integrity of your toys. Here is a quick review:

- **Water-based lube:** Can be used on any toy! It doesn't degrade toys, is safe for bodily contact, and keeps things slick.

- **Silicone-based lube:** Should be used on toys made of hard substances (like glass, marble, and hard plastic). DO NOT use on silicone or jelly-based toys—the silicone molecules from each will want to join together, resulting in no lubrication.

- **Oil-based lubes:** Do not use on toys. Getting oil off of the toy will require using harsh, alcohol-based substances that may degrade it.

- **Tip:** Make sure your sex toys are of superior quality—you are worth it! Buy from reputable vendors and be sure they are phthalate- and BPA-free.

# Rookies: When It's Your First Time

It is very important to have a positive experience the first time you have sex with your spouse. If your first time together happens to be on your honeymoon, even better! Your honeymoon can be the perfect environment for your first intimate experience. You are able to forget about your daily stresses and focus on each other. Whether you are both new to sex, only one of you is, or you are just new to each other, this Playbook will help make your first sexual experience together an enjoyable memory you'll want to repeat again and again... and again! These basic tips will help your first experience.

- **Be patient:** You may not get things right the first time. That's ok! Stay positive, and help each other out.

- **Don't underestimate the power and necessity of foreplay:** Most women need lots of foreplay to become physically aroused. As a woman gets aroused, her vagina begins to lubricate and tents open, making penetration much more pleasurable. Men need to relax, and be in the moment without performance expectations.

- **Use lube:** When things are wet, it is more enjoyable for both partners. Using extra lube can take the pressure off her to become wet, and make things more comfortable for both of you. If you are using condoms, make sure to use water-based lube.

- **Keep your sense of humor:** Don't be afraid to slow down, talk, and share a laugh if things feel awkward or don't work out as expected. Improvise and be creative!!

- **Communicate:** If something feels great, tell your partner! If something feels not so great, tell your partner! Communication is especially important as you learn about each other's preferences and let them know yours. Remember to be positive.

*"It is very likely that a woman's hymen, (known to be a membrane that covers the vagina) can be partially closed, stretched, or torn and in fact, may be broken long before she has intercourse for the first time. So, don't expect to "pop" anything other than champagne bottles!"*

Have fun, and enjoy each other in these special moments!

## Coming Up Short (or Not Coming at All): Common Sexual Issues and How to Solve Them

### Down for the Count or Going Flaccid: How to Get Back Up Again

Many men lose their erection at some time during sex. It is not necessarily a reflection of their enjoyment, attraction to their partner, or even anything sexual! Stress, drugs, anxiety, alcohol, and hormone levels can all cause an erection to go flaccid. Often, the issue is simply mental. If it happens, just relax. Worrying about it will only make it worse, so be in the moment and feel every sensation. Think of the friction, the heat, the skin on skin, or your sensations. If that does not help, ask your partner if you can pleasure them to take pressure off yourself. Keep things light: "My sergeant just can't stand at attention right now," or "Let's give him a break right now, and let me focus on you!" If you are too shy to say that, remember there are no rules about when you have to be erect or the order in which you have sex. If things aren't looking "up," just go back to the foreplay section of this book or try a sex game or two.

### Shooting Early

Early ejaculation is one of the most common sexual issues men face, and it can happen at any stage of their sexual lives. Neither one of you should worry if it happens. After a little downtime, most men are able to get hard and go again. Plus, if she's already had an orgasm there is no such thing as "too soon." Vulvas do not need much of a recovery period—all the more reason to get back to foreplay! Sex doesn't have to end when the man orgasms. Oral and manual stimulation can result in multiple orgasms for her and a fun rest break for him. Keep playing, and things will start looking "up" again!

## Not Properly Warmed Up?

### Tackling Dryness

Stress, anxiety, medication, and alcohol can all interfere with a woman's natural lubrication production. Keeping things nice and wet will make everything much more enjoyable, not to mention less painful for both of you. So don't skimp on the lube, and do reapply repeatedly. Use all natural, water-based lube—nothing with scents or sweeteners—to avoid a potentially itchy or painful reaction.

### Make Sure She is in the Game

It is important to note that wetness is not the sole indicator of arousal. When a woman is ready, her clitoris will be engorged and erect. The more engorged and erect she is, the more pleasure she will receive, so remember that during your sex play! Make sure one of you has access to her clitoris with a hand or sex toy to hit all of her pleasure nerves. Orgasms that come (pun intended!) as a result of both vaginal and clitoral stimulation for some can be the most intense and are called "blended orgasms."

**Addressing the Pain**

There are several factors that may cause a woman to feel pain during intercourse. Medical conditions such as vaginismus, endometriosis, and genital infections can cause this, however pain is frequently a result of:

Lack of foreplay (kissing, touching, teasing, and nonpenetrative genital stimulation):

Without enough foreplay, the vagina won't produce enough juices to keep things wet, and may not tent open enough to comfortably fit fingers, toys, or a penis. If things get painful because of dryness, or you didn't start with lots of foreplay, add lots of lube! (And then add some more lube)

Pressure on the cervix:

A sharp pain may indicate that the cervix is being hit. In positions like doggy-style, this is a common experience. Try switching positions such as woman-on-top and spooning (on your sides), as both offer great sensations without overly deep penetration.

Men may also experience pain during intercourse. This may be due to a lack of lubrication causing uncomfortable chafing on their penis, or medical conditions such as inflammation of the prostate, urinary tract infections, or dermatitis.

If pain during intercourse persists for either of you, it is important to see a doctor.

## When Things Get Too Intense

If either of you experiences any pain or feels the sensations are too intense, take a break. It is important to realize that some activities create laughter and some generate tears. Talk with your spouse about these. Try using your mouth or fingertips on less sensitive arms or body parts, or get into some deep kissing (check out page 71 for some kissing tips!). Although the closeness of penetration offers a beautiful feeling of connection, sex isn't always about "penis in vagina."

## Game Tunes: M-C's Sexy Playlist

Do you have a sexy playlist made for your honeymoon? Everybody has their own taste in music. Please feel free to test out mine. The first one is my favorite and I can't believe I first heard it on the radio (1976).

- Je t'aime, moi non plus by *Serge Gainsbourg and Jane Berkin*
- Pillowtalk by *Zayne*
- No Ordinary Love by *Sade*
- Touch My Body by *Mariah Carey*
- Get You by *Daniel Caesar*
- Doing It by *LL Cool J*
- Good For You by *Selena James*
- Skin by *Rihanna*
- Adorn by *Miguel*
- Pony by *Ginuwine*

# APPENDIX B

## Travel Advice

**1.** Reconfirm all trip details (e.g. flights, rental cars, hotels) before you leave and print or have electronic copies with you. Travel agents will tell you it is especially important to confirm flight details as there are often last-minute airline schedule changes.

**2.** Flying? Check the baggage weight limit and pack a little lighter if you plan on doing some honeymoon shopping! If you do not own a baggage scale, hop on the scale with the bag in your hand and subtract your weight from the total. Double check whether you have any liquids or aerosols in containers and that they adhere to airline guidelines. Make sure they are placed in a sealable medium sized baggie. (Don't have a baggie? Don't worry. Bags are often provided free at airports prior to security).

**3.** Pack your carry-on carefully: bring an extra set of clothes and your valuables (including sex toys) in case your checked bag gets delayed, and include all medications such as birth control.

**4.** Remember to pack not only your bathing suit and adventure clothes, but also your daily surprise kits and presents.

**5.** Travel with medical insurance. Better safe than sorry! Many travel credit cards allow for additional baggage and trip delay or interruption insurance. Check out your policies in advance and purchase more coverage if needed.

**6.** Get your frequent flyer and travel point cards credited when booking or checking in. Let your credit card company know you are travelling.

# Adventure Honeymoon Travel Tips

Adventure can bring you closer together than you can imagine—the thrill of experiencing something new with someone you love is very special. Taking an "adventure style" honeymoon (or just an adventure on your honeymoon) will not only give you amazing memories to cherish for years to come, but it can also deepen your spousal connection. Although adventures are great at any time in a relationship, your honeymoon is an excellent time to dive into something exciting.

But first, you and your spouse need to decide what "adventure" means. Does it mean taking a few small excursions on your all-inclusive beach holiday, or does it mean backpacking through the Amazon? Once you are both on the same page about what kind of adventure you want to take, you can lay out your expectations of the trip and research any "must-do" activities or experiences. Although spontaneity during your adventure is encouraged, the initial planning stages should be agreed upon and well thought out to avoid disappointment. Remember your spouse is the priority on your honeymoon, not the adventure itself!

Follow these tips to help make your honeymoon the adventure of a lifetime:

**Safeguard Passports, Money, ID, Important items**
Make sure to review your passports and visas at least three months before your trip to ensure expiration dates meet the travel requirements of the country you are visiting.

Spread out your important documents (drivers licences, insurance, credit cards, etc.) and take a photo of each with your cell phone so if you lose something, you have a record of the information handy. As backup, you may want to make copies and keep them in a separate location in your luggage from the originals. Always keep your original documents in a safe place while you travel.

Bring extra cash in the local currency, (purchased in advance or at most airports) and keep small amounts in various locations. Take photos of other important or valuable items you are bringing in case they are stolen, and you need to file an insurance claim.

## Pay Attention to Pace

If you just got married, you may need a day or two to recover from the wedding excitement. Try not to schedule too many activities at the beginning of your trip to help you recover from any long flight jet lag, or just exhaustion. You may also appreciate a day or two at the end of your trip to lay low with your spouse and bask in the glow of your honeymoon adventure. Check in with your spouse throughout the trip to see if the pace is too hectic (or not enough), and adjust accordingly.

## Pack an Emergency Kit

Bring an emergency health kit. Dr. Jaclyn, Naturopathic Doctor recommends bringing the following:

- **Jet Lag:** Melatonin 1-10 mg, thirty minutes before bed (dose based on tolerance). Upon departure, take the melatonin in accordance with the sleep schedule you would like to have at your destination. Once you've arrived, continue taking the melatonin until you feel you are back on track. Follow the same guidelines for your return journey.

- **Trauma/Injuries/Nausea/Vomiting/Inflammation/Infection:** Take Bryonia Smiliaplex (by Pascoe) 10-15 drops up to 10x/day as needed.

- **Scrapes/Wounds:** Calendula cream applied topically 2-3x/day (avoid use with deep wounds).

- **Oregano Oil:** 1 drop/day to support your immune system, 3-5 drops/day if you develop an infection. Take separately from probiotics by at least two hours.

- **Probiotics:** 10 billion/day to prevent digestive disorders, 30-50 billion/day for treatment. If you have access to a fridge, use refrigerated probiotics (this supplement can survive eight to twelve hours unrefrigerated while you travel). If you don't have access to a fridge, get a shelf-stable probiotic.

**Stay Positive**

On any adventure, things might not go exactly as planned. Remain positive! Try to flow with, and respond to changes by brainstorming solutions together instead of reacting negatively to something that is out of your control. Even better, take advantage of the situation by making it fun: if you missed a bus or a flight connection, book a couples' massage, try a local restaurant, or take an impromptu stroll where you are. Look around, or ask locals, to find out what might be fun. By expecting the unexpected and reacting positively, you'll be able to enjoy the hiccups instead of being frustrated.

**Get Out of Your Comfort Zone**

Try some crazy stuff! Take a helicopter ride. Jump out of a plane or bungee jump! Bring pencils and pens for local children. Meet a local family and learn about their culture and/or how they live. Ask each other what would make this trip one that you will NEVER forget, and plan a (mini) adventure bucket list. Use your imagination; is that sunset hot air balloon ride simply not possible? Climb to a lookout point and have your own sunset champagne toast, no balloon ride required. Be mindful of your spouse's preferences while you're experiencing these adventures: always be each other's cheerleaders! (e.g. "I can't get over how brave you were when I saw you take off on that zip line.")

### Pack Light

Pack light, and then try to cut what you've packed in half, adding back essentials only. Bring clothes that can be hand washed and drip dried overnight. Shampoo is usually pH balanced, so you can use it to do a small quick hand wash of your clothing if needed.

### Look Around

Before you leave a location, look in every single drawer and corner of your rooms—you may be leaving something valuable behind!

*"I love packing my things in small see-through bags (with zippers). That way I can quickly locate what I need, and put things in each dedicated space right away. There are even plastic bags that let out all of the air so that you can fit more in the bag, (but be mindful of your luggage weight maximum)."*

### Check Out Travel and Health Insurance

As adventure honeymooners, you will appreciate the security and peace of mind of having travel and health insurance in place. Check your company, personal, and other insurance to make sure you are covered, and supplement with a trip-specific policy if needed.

### Go Heavy on the PDA (Public Displays of Affection)

Hug and kiss as often as possible: in elevators, alleys, and mountaintops as long as this is socially acceptable at your destination. As a matter of fact, make a point of finding the most adventurous places to do so, and be sure to record it via selfie. Don't worry about looking like a touristy honeymoon couple—embrace it (literally!).

Make a game out of seeing if you can outdo yourselves every day, and up the ante on the funniest or most interesting places you can find. Many studies report that hugging, touching, and kissing in public is a key to staying connected in your marriage. Making PDA's happen during your honeymoon will be purely magical.

**Own Your Honeymooner Status**

If you are not shy, tell everyone that you are on your honeymoon. You will build instant bonds with others and receive many well wishes, special treatment, and maybe a few upgrades!

*"A couple I met while we were in Vietnam told me many hotels upgraded them to honeymoon suites at no extra charge. On a small overnight cruise, the crew ordered them a beautiful flower bouquet which the groom presented to his wife. At dinner while the crew sang a romantic song, they also received very fancy (and free) cocktails."*

**Unplug**

Leave your destination information with key family members and work associates, and then cut yourself off from them (no e-mails, calls, social media, etc.). Be clear that you should only be contacted for emergencies. Focusing on each other and the special adventures you have planned will ensure a deeper spousal connection. You can upload your photos and communicate with everyone when you get back home, so live in the moment.

# Complete Trip Checklist

**Clothing:**

- ☐ lingerie
- ☐ hats
- ☐ pants
- ☐ dresses
- ☐ shorts
- ☐ belts
- ☐ skirts
- ☐ socks
- ☐ underwear
- ☐ jacket
- ☐ raincoat
- ☐ sweaters
- ☐ bathing suits and cover
- ☐ shirts
- ☐ scarves
- ☐ workout clothes
- ☐ shoes/sandals
- ☐ workout shoes
- ☐ dress shoes
- ☐ suit

**Toiletries:**

- ☐ makeup
- ☐ razor & cream
- ☐ shampoo & conditioner
- ☐ toothbrush
- ☐ toothpaste
- ☐ deodorant
- ☐ hair dryer
- ☐ curling iron
- ☐ hair straightener
- ☐ hairbrush & comb
- ☐ hair accessories
- ☐ creams & lotions
- ☐ glasses
- ☐ 2 pairs of sunglasses
- ☐ contacts & solution
- ☐ tampons, diva cup, etc.
- ☐ birth control
- ☐ coconut or other massage oil (remember oils can compromise the integrity of a condom)
- ☐ medication (in your carry on!)
- ☐ supplements & vitamins
- ☐ tweezers & nail files
- ☐ sunscreen
- ☐ insect repellent
- ☐ aloe
- ☐ vitamin E for scrapes, cuts, etc.
- ☐ small first aid kit

## Extras:

- ☐ headphones for carry-on
- ☐ all chargers
- ☐ fully charged cell phone (prearrange a calling plan with your carrier)
- ☐ laptop or tablet
- ☐ camera
- ☐ electrical converters & adapters
- ☐ alarm clock
- ☐ purse & money belt
- ☐ books & magazines
- ☐ sewing kit
- ☐ water bottle (carry on)
- ☐ travel pillow
- ☐ backpack, beach bag, etc.
- ☐ sleep mask
- ☐ umbrella
- ☐ emergency bracelet or ID in pocket
- ☐ sex toys for him AND her!

## Guides and Documents:

- ☐ travel guides
- ☐ passport (check expiration)
- ☐ photocopy of passport, placed in a separate bag
- ☐ credit cards & cash in local currency
- ☐ tickets
- ☐ itinerary
- ☐ maps
- ☐ insurance (some travel credit cards offer extra insurance)
- ☐ medical info
- ☐ contact list

## Winter Honeymoon Extras:

- ☐ boots
- ☐ gloves/mittens
- ☐ hats
- ☐ warm socks
- ☐ snow suits
- ☐ toe/hand warmers
- ☐ warm underwear

# Sex Stuff

- ☐ water- based lubricant
- ☐ massage oil
- ☐ two large poster rolls or pieces of newspaper end roll large enough to trace each other's body
- ☐ colorful markers
- ☐ feather or a ticklish item like a soft brush
- ☐ deck of cards
- ☐ one spoon
- ☐ paper, pen, soft ties & scarves
- ☐ two hats or creative containers
- ☐ a plastic sheet (shower curtain works)
- ☐ nontoxic and nonstaining foam or paint
- ☐ underwear you are not attached to
- ☐ two water guns
- ☐ two white T-shirts
- ☐ two blindfolds
- ☐ lingerie for her
- ☐ sexy underwear for him
- ☐ one Nerf gun and ammo or socks rolled up in a ball
- ☐ small bullet vibrator
- ☐ sleeve or stroker toy

# Appendix C - Body Map

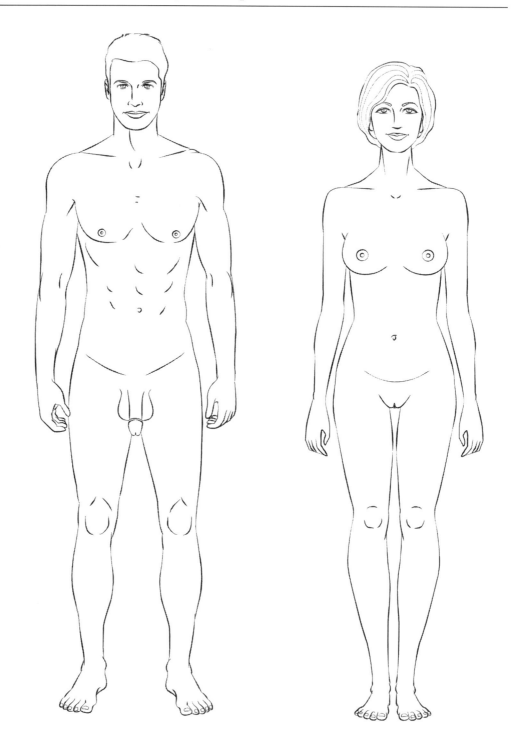

**LEGEND:**   1 = Dislike   2 = Neutral   3 = Pleasurable   **4 = Orgasmic!**

# Appendix C - Body Map

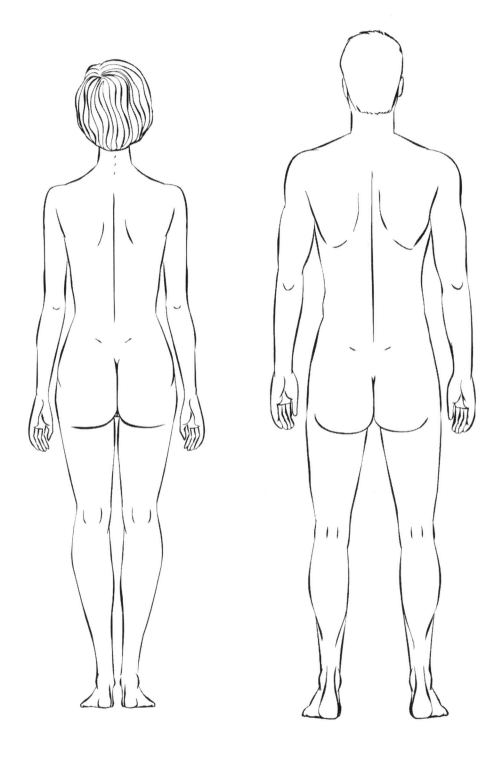

**LEGEND:** 1 = Dislike   2 = Neutral   3 = Pleasurable   **4 = Orgasmic!**

# Bibliography

Acevedo, B.P., Aron, A., Fisher, H.E., & Brown, L.L. (2012). Neural correlates of long-term intense romantic love. *SocCogn Affect Neurosci 7(2).* Retrieved May 1, 2018, from https://www.ncbi.nlm.nih.gov/pubmed/21208991?dopt=Abstract

Allison, S. (2004). *Tickle His Pickle: Your hands-on guide to penis pleasing.* San Francisco, CA: Tickle Kitty Inc.

Ben-Zeév, A. (2013). *Why Make-Up Sex and Breakup Sex Are So Good.* Retrieved May 1, 2018, from https://www.psychologytoday.com/blog/in-the-name-love/201302/why-make-sex-and-breakup-sex-are-so-good

Byers, S. (2011). Beyond the Birds and the Bees and Was It Good for You?: Thirty Years of Research on Sexual Communication. *Canadian Psychology, 52(1).* Retrieved May 1, 2018, from http://connection.ebscohost.com/c/articles/59414911/beyond-birds-bees-was-good-you-thirty-years-research-sexual-communication

Field T., Hernandez-Reif M., Diego M., Schanberg S., Kuhn C. (2005). Cortisol decreases and serotonin and dopamine increase following massage therapy. *Int J Neurosci., 115(10).* Retrieved May 1, 2018, from https://www.ncbi.nlm.nih.gov/pubmed/16162447/

Miller, A. (2013). Can this marriage be saved? *American Psychological Association, 44(4).* Retrieved May 1, 2018 from http://www.apa.org/monitor/2013/04/marriage.aspx

Montesi, J. (2011). The specific importance of communicating about sex to couples' sexual and overall relationship satisfaction. *Journal of Social and Personal Relationships, 28(5).* Retrieved May 1, 2018, from http://spr.sagepub.com/content/28/5/591.abstract

# Honeymoon Notes:

17422099R00107

Made in the USA
Lexington, KY
19 November 2018